ALI

Thunder Bay Press
An imprint of the Baker & Taylor Publishing Group
10350 Barnes Canyon Road, San Diego, CA 92121
www.thunderbaybooks.com

All notations of errors or omissions should be addressed to Thunder Bay Press,
Editorial Department, at the above address. All other correspondence (author
inquiries, permissions) concerning the content of this book should be addressed
to Moseley Road, Inc., 123 Main Street, Irvington, NY 10533.
www.moseleyroad.com.

ISBN-13: 978-1-60710-569-5
ISBN-10: 1-60710-569-1

Printed in China

1 2 3 4 5 16 15 14 13 12

ALI

THE OFFICIAL PORTRAIT OF "THE GREATEST" OF ALL TIME

CONTENTS

Ali is jubilant after defeating Sonny Liston to take the heavyweight crown.

INTRODUCTION

"Ali! Ali! Ali!"

Boxing is simple. It plays out like the rules in *Thunderdome*—two men enter, one man leaves. Sometimes one fighter wins, sometimes the other fighter wins, sometimes it's a draw. (Sometimes someone takes a dive, but that's a story for a whole other book!)

Yet within this simple sport lie primal archetypes that stir the soul: the champ and the challenger, the hero and the bully, the underdog and the favorite, the slugger and the strategist, the crowd pleaser and the come-from-behind kid. And the thing that makes boxing such a complex sport, in spite of being so simple in theory, is that any of these roles can—and do—alter from fight to fight. Yet even in a sport where the rooting factor has always been as changeable as the weather, only one boxer has simultaneously been viewed as both a prince and a pariah: the heavyweight fighter who was introduced to the world of boxing as Cassius Clay, and who changed it as Muhammad Ali.

For years after Clay adopted his new name and pointedly asked to be addressed as Muhammad Ali, magazines and newspapers continued to write, "Cassius Clay, now known as Muhammad Ali" or some similar addendum. And then they wondered why he was an angry young black man. But that was the public's paradox: they wanted to adore him but refused to respect him. And he wanted to fight for them but refused to kill for them . . . and so that was his paradox.

Had he been less magnificent, less capable of fulfilling every brag and boast and Seussically rhymed threat, he would have been no more than a passing novelty act. But he turned out to be what biologists call a "sport"—an animal that is not like any that came before it. Compared to most other fighters, Ali was taller, faster, and more agile. He had an extraordinary reach, the resilience to take a punch, and the quicksilver speed to deliver one unseen.

He also delighted in turning the tables on his critics. His teachers (and his draft board) told him he wasn't smart; yet people quote him every day. Trainers told him he didn't box properly; yet he is the only lineal three-time heavyweight champion. When the government told him he could no longer climb into a boxing ring, he climbed onto a soapbox and eventually KOed the Feds.

And while it's true his arrival reinvigorated a floundering sport that was lamenting the retirement of its former legends—Joe Walcott, Sugar Ray Robinson, and Rocky Marciano—and desperately seeking new ones, his stature became so unassailable that he made it hard for any other fighters to become legends in their own right. Even at the pallid end of his career, when fans were lucky to see fleeting glimpses of his former grace and skill, they still chanted, "Ali! Ali! Ali!"

Muhammad Ali in 1963, at the start of a tumultuous career that brought him both fame and infamy—and that ultimately brought him true greatness.

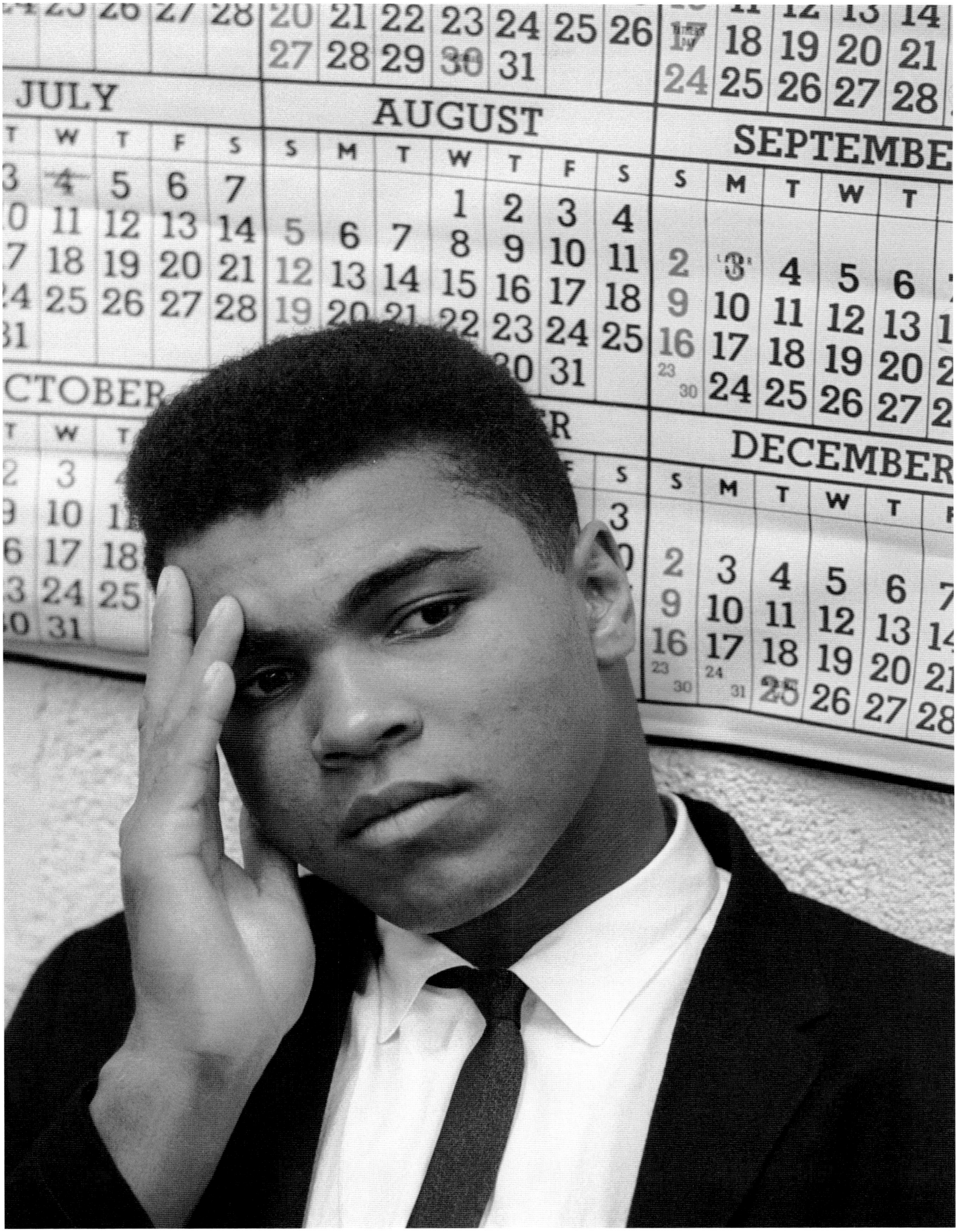
JULY
AUGUST
SEPTEMBE
DECEMBER

Never at a loss for words, Ali
speaks with reporters after
landing at Heathrow in 1966.

CHAPTER ONE

YOUNG CASSIUS CLAY

"When I was growing up, too many colored people thought it was better to be white. And I don't know what it was, but I always felt like I was born to do something for my people."

In 1954, at the start of his career, a pensive-looking, 12-year-old Cassius Clay adopts his orthodox boxing stance.

THE STOLEN BICYCLE

"Champions aren't made in the gyms. Champions are made from something they have deep inside them—a desire, a dream, a vision."

It all started with a bike.

In October 1954, a twelve-year-old boy named Cassius Clay rode his bicycle down to a merchant's fair being held at the Columbia Auditorium in Louisville, Kentucky. After he'd had his fill of the food and fun inside, he went outside to discover that his new red-and-white Schwinn had been stolen. Upset and angry, Clay went looking for someone to help him recover his bicycle and exact his revenge. As luck would have it, he ran across police officer Joe Martin, who trained young boxers in his spare time. When the boy insisted that he was going to "whup" the person who stole his bike, Officer Martin suggested that he learn to fight first before making such threats. The seed was planted then and there.

LEFT: The former Columbia Auditorium building now houses the Spalding University Center, but it was here at the Louisville Service Club's black merchant bazaar that Clay's journey to championship began.

RIGHT: Clay training in the gym with his younger brother, Rudolph. Like his brother, Rudolph converted to Islam, taking the name Rahman Ali. The Clay brothers boxed together in an amateur league, but it was only Cassius who was selected for the U.S. Olympic team. Rudolph remained an amateur until his brother became heavyweight champion after beating Sonny Liston. As a professional boxer, he won fourteen fights, seven by knockouts, and lost three.

GROWING UP IN LOUISVILLE

"Wars of nations are fought to change maps.
But wars of poverty are fought to map change."

Cassius Marcellus Clay Jr. came into the world on January 17, 1942, and grew up in a middle-class family in the then-struggling city of Louisville, famous for the Kentucky Derby and baseball's Louisville Sluggers. Young Cassius had just one sibling, a younger brother, Rudolph Valentino Clay. His family wasn't poor but, as writer Toni Morrison points out, the Clays weren't in the best situation either. "Black middle class, black Southern middle class," she writes, "is not white middle class at all."

Although the boy was named after his father, Cassius Marcellus Clay was a family name going back many generations to a white man, a famous abolitionist. Cassius Sr., who worked as a mural painter, was a heavy drinker, and the household was not always a peaceful one. Cassius Jr. wasn't a particularly good student, but he must have picked up something during class—as his vocabulary, clever wordplay, quick wit, and poise as an adult would later attest.

During the boy's formative years, the city was still in the grip of segregation, meaning African Americans were discriminated against and had to use separate facilities, often ones that were substandard compared to white facilities. Cassius

BELOW: The Kentucky Derby held at Churchill Downs in Louisville, Kentucky, in 1942, the year Cassius Clay was born.

would not have been able to sit in the lower level of the movie house, drink from a "white" water fountain or use the indoor restroom in a store. It is convenient to imagine that he was a carefree young boy who accepted the times he lived in and rarely felt troubled by these issues, but one incident he related tells another story. When he read about the 1955 racial murder in Mississippi of Emmett Till—a black youth about his age— Cassius reacted by angrily hurling stones at an "UNCLE SAM WANTS YOU" enlistment poster.

ABOVE: Clay grew up in the segregated South, where as a child he'd become very familiar with the signs that designated which areas were for white use only, such as at this bus terminal.

ODESSA CLAY:
A MOTHER IN A MILLION

"She's a sweet, fat, wonderful woman, who loves to cook, eat, make clothes, and be with family. She doesn't drink, smoke, meddle in other people's business, or bother anyone, and there's no one who's been better to me my whole life."

Christine Martin, the widow of Clay's first trainer, Joe Martin, often helped get her husband's young boxers to the fights. "I would drive those boys everywhere," she explained in an interview with the Louisville *Courier-Journal*. "Cassius was a very easy-to-get-along-with fellow. Very easy to handle. Very polite. Whatever you asked him to do, that's what he'd do. His mother, that's why. She was a wonderful person."

Odessa Lee Clay (*nee* Grady) was born in 1917 in Hopkins County, Kentucky. Her paternal grandfather was a white Irish emigrant named Abe Grady who married Amanda Walker of Todd County, Kentucky. Her maternal grandfather, Tom Morehead, was the son of a white man named Morehead and a black slave named Dinah; he served with the United States Colored Troops during the Civil War.

At the age of sixteen, Odessa met and married mural painter and piano player Cassius Clay, called "Cash," and they settled in a house in Louisville. The marriage was an uneasy one, and the boxer admitted to confidants that his mother was afraid of his father. Odessa was a devout Baptist who shared her faith with her two sons, Cassius and Rudolph. She brought them to church every Sunday and made sure that they knew the Bible. Ali said of his mother, whom he affectionately called "Bird"—"She taught us to love people and treat everyone with kindness. I've changed my religion and some of my beliefs since then, but her God is still God. I just call Him by a different name."

Odessa loyally followed her son's boxing career and often traveled great distances to be ringside at his fights. Also, as his trusted confidant, she helped to support him through many of his dark times—both personal and professional.

She died of heart failure in 1994, fours years after the passing of her husband.

Clay plants a kiss on his mother, Odessa Lee Clay.

LEARNING TO FIGHT

"I had it in my heart. I believed in myself, and I had confidence. I knew how to do it, I had natural talent, and I pursued it."

Under Joe Martin's tutelage, Clay immediately took to boxing, working out at the Louisville Columbia gym with other young would-be pugilists. Martin even featured him on his TV show, *Tomorrow's Champions.* Clay also worked with an African American trainer, Fred Stoner, who taught the boy the "sweet science" of boxing and coached him on how to move with the fluid grace of a dancer. (During the last four years of Clay's amateur career, he trained with legendary boxing cutman Chuck Bodak.)

Six weeks into his training, Clay climbed into the ring for his first amateur bout against another unseasoned fighter named Ronnie O'Keefe. The fight consisted of three one-minute rounds, and Clay earned his first win via a split decision. Two years later, at age fourteen (and trained by Fred Stoner), he won the first of six Kentucky Golden Gloves titles fighting in the light heavyweight division. He'd add two National Golden Gloves titles and a pair of national Amateur Athletic Union crowns to his growing list of achievements. In all, he racked up a hundred amateur wins by the time he was eighteen. Despite his many accomplishments, Clay wasn't exactly gaining national notoriety, but all of that was about to change.

Clay knocked out Gary Jawish in Madison Square Garden in 1960 during the Golden Gloves competition.

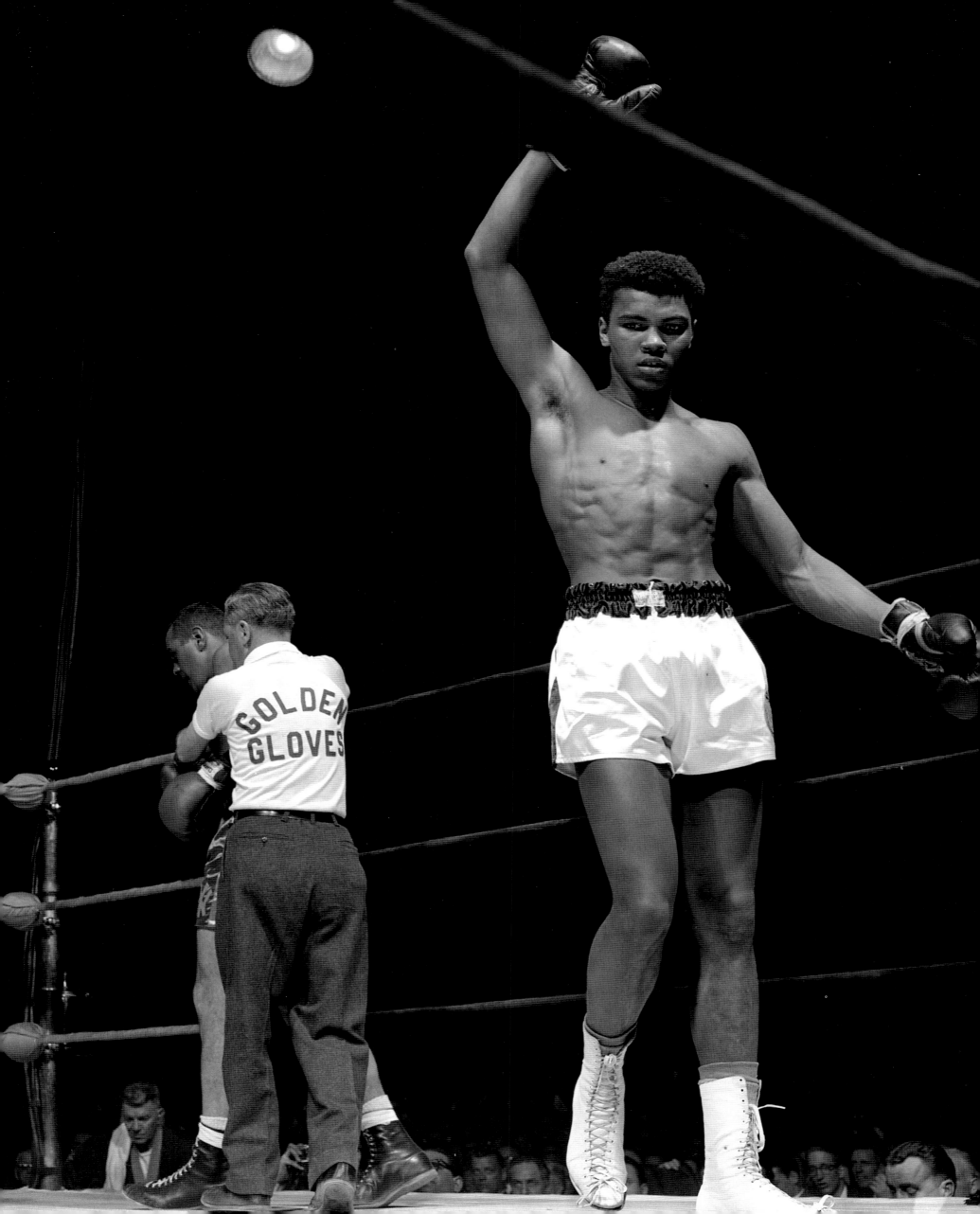

THE 1960 OLYMPICS

"To make America the greatest is my goal,
So I beat the Russian, and I beat the Pole,
And for the USA won the Medal of gold.
Italians said, 'You're Greater than the Cassius of old.'
We like your name, we like your game,
So make Rome your home if you will.
I said I appreciate your kind hospitality,
But the USA is my country still,
'Cause they're waiting to welcome me in Louisville."

—1960, AFTER WINNING THE OLYMPIC GOLD MEDAL IN ROME

The 1960 Summer Olympic boxing trials were to be held in San Francisco, and Clay was one of the young men chosen to compete for a spot on the U.S. men's boxing team. There was one little problem, though: he was deathly afraid of flying. Someone suggested that he could take a train, but the Olympics were taking place in Rome that summer, meaning all competing athletes had to fly overseas. Joe Martin and others eventually prevailed upon Clay to take the flight to California, but not before he went out and bought himself a parachute to bring on board. He made it to San Francisco in one piece and earned a place on the Olympic team as a light heavyweight.

Eddie Crook (left), Cassius Clay (middle), and Skeeter McClure (right), each won a gold medal in boxing at the 1960 Olympics.

"I'm gonna have to be killed before I lose, and I ain't going to die easy."

Cassius Clay unleashes a fierce right hook in his victory over Gennadiy Shatov of the Soviet Union to win a gold medal in the light-heavyweight division.

In Rome, Clay was the toast of the Olympic Village and a force to be reckoned with in the ring. As a U.S. Olympic Committee spokesperson put it, "In the ring, he murders 'em with his fists. Outside the ring he kills them with kindness . . ."

Clay won his first bout against Belgian Yvon Becaus on a second-round stoppage by the referee. In his next fight, he took a unanimous decision from Gennadiy Shatov of Russia. He earned another unanimous decision in his third contest, this time versus Australian Tony Madigan. Then the only man left standing between Clay and the gold medal was Zbigniew Pietrzykowski of Poland. A bronze medalist in the 1956 games, Pietrzykowski landed some solid blows in the opening round as Clay struggled to cope with his left-handed opponent. The second round was less eventful, but Clay would later say that he knew that he would need a big third round to win the fight. He got it. Clay peppered Pietrzykowski with rights and lefts in the final round and won a unanimous decision. He would return home an Olympic hero, so proud of his gold medal that he didn't take it off for two days. The kid with the stolen bike was now a fighter on a roll.

"I came back to Louisville after the Olympics with my shiny gold medal. Went into a luncheonette where black folks couldn't eat. Thought I'd put them on the spot. I sat down and asked for a meal. The Olympic champion wearing his gold medal. They said, "We don't serve niggers here." I said, "That's okay, I don't eat 'em." But they put me out in the street. So I went down to the river, the Ohio River, and threw my gold medal in it."

Clay smiles during the Olympic medal ceremony in Rome. He was soon disenchanted though with the racism he still faced at home, even after bringing honor to his country. He later said "A black man in America can win an Olympic gold medal, but he can't even come home and be served a hamburger."

FROM GOLD MEDAL TO FAST CASH

"To be able to give away riches is mandatory if you wish to possess them. This is the only way that you will be truly rich."

The city fathers of Louisville made much of their native son when he returned with Olympic gold. Shortly thereafter, Cassius Clay signed a deal with a syndicate of wealthy white investors known as the Louisville Sponsoring Group, who gave him a $10,000 signing bonus in exchange for a percentage of his earnings as a professional fighter. One of the first things he did with this windfall was make a down payment on a new Cadillac.

The sponsors summed up how Louisville felt about Clay's potential in the following statement: "Each of the ten members of the group has admiration for Cassius Clay as a fine young man and confidence in his ability as a boxer. The principal purpose of the group is to provide hometown support for Cassius' professional career and to aid him in realizing the maximum benefits from his efforts."

Clay meets with the Louisville Sponsoring Group in 1963.

COPING WITH THE SPECTER OF SEGREGATION

"I know I got it made while the masses of black people are catchin' hell, but as long as they ain't free, I ain't free."

During his stay in Rome at the Olympic Village, Clay had seen athletes from many nations come together in the unified spirit of the games. He'd met and mingled with men and women of many ethnicities and many varied beliefs. When he got home to Louisville, however, he was met with that sorry remnant of the Jim Crow South called segregation. Even as an Olympic champion, he was forbidden to enter certain businesses or recreational facilities. Again, he was beginning to see the unfairness of the social system in some parts of America. When he was actually refused service at an "all-white" restaurant, he began to feel like a second-class citizen instead of a hometown hero. To protest this double standard, which judged a man by his skin color before it acknowledged his achievements, Clay stood on the Jefferson County Bridge and threw his Olympic medal into the Ohio River. Awards and accolades, he reasoned, meant nothing if they changed so little of your everyday life. It was almost as though he knew that a significant change was coming, one that would alter his life—and boxing career—forever.

In the early 1960s African Americans were still segregated from their white compatriots in many states and were restricted to inferior facilities and services in housing, medical care, education, employment, and transportation.

GORGEOUS GEORGE
AND THE LOUISVILLE LIP

"I'm beautiful. I'm so pretty that if a
sucker touches my face, I'll kill him.
If he messes with my hair,
I'll pummel him."

— GORGEOUS GEORGE

Clay knew almost instinctively that he needed something novel to set him apart from other fighters. He took stock of his attributes and was not disappointed: in addition to being a talented fighter, he was a handsome young man with a winning smile and a wicked sense of humor. But he still wasn't sure how that was going to get him noticed in the competitive world of professional prizefighting.

Then, at a wrestling match in Las Vegas, Ali saw the novelty wrestler "Gorgeous George" Wagner for the first time. Wagner, "the man you love to hate," had gained fame for his over-the-top preening, for calling himself "pretty" and "beautiful," and for saying insulting or demeaning things about his opponents. In Gorgeous George's own words, if he loses to an opponent, "I'll crawl across the ring and cut my hair off! But that's not gonna happen because

I'm the greatest wrestler in the world!"

Clay himself thought Gorgeous George was ridiculous, but he also noticed the arena was full of paying customers who roared in gleeful anticipation when the platinum-curled George—clad in a garish satin robe—climbed into the ring.

Ali recalled, "I saw 15,000 people comin' to see this man get beat. And his talking did it. The lightbulb flashed on in Clay's brain. I said, "This is a gooood idea!" And so his signature strategy was born: talk up your boxing skills, talk up your pretty face, then verbally slam your opponent over and over . . . and do it all with swagger and style.

Ali's bragging gained him so much media attention that he was finally offered a title bout against Liston, even though he was not the top-ranked contender.

Gorgeous George wrestling
in a Chicago ring in 1949.

"I figured that if I said it enough, I would convince the world that I really was the greatest."

RIGHT: Gorgeous George dressed like a king for his ringside appearances.

OPPOSITE PAGE: Clay parades around the ring with a crown and robe before his fight with Henry Cooper in 1963.

LIFE MAGAZINE

Neil Leifer, possibly the best sports photographer of his day, covered Ali for *Time* and *Sports Illustrated* from the early 1960s through the end of his career. Here, he tells the remarkable story behind Muhammad's famed underwater shoot:

How good was Ali at self-promotion? Let me tell you a story that shows his genius. After he turned pro, *Sports Illustrated* did a piece on him. They assigned a freelance photographer named Flip Schulke, and Ali—he was Cassius Clay then— asked, "Who do you work for?" Schulke told him he did a lot of work for *Life*. This was when *Life* was the biggest magazine in the country, and Ali wasn't that big then. He'd won the gold medal, but that was it. There was no reason for Ali to be in *Life* magazine, so when he said, "Man, how about shooting me for *Life*?" Schulke told him, "I'd love to, but I'd never get it past the editors." Well, Ali accepted that, but a few minutes later, he was asking questions again. "Tell me about some of the photography you've done." And Schulke explained that he did a lot of underwater photography; that was his specialty. And Ali thought of something on the spur of the moment, which shows what an absolute genius he was. His eyes widened, and he told Schulke, "I never told anyone this, but me and Angelo have a secret. Do you know why I'm the fastest heavyweight in the world? I'm the only heavyweight that trains underwater." Schulke said "What do you mean?" And Ali explained, "You know why fighters wear heavy shoes when they run? They wear those shoes because, when you take them off and put other shoes on, you feel real light and you run real fast. Well, I get in the water up to my neck, and I punch in the water, and then when I get out of the water, I'm lightning fast because there's no resistance." Schulke was skeptical, but Ali swore it was the truth, and to prove his point, he told Schulke, "Tomorrow morning with Angelo, and no one's ever seen it before. I'll let you photograph it for *Life* magazine as an exclusive." So Schulke called up *Life* and suggested the piece, and I think they ran five pages of Ali up to his neck in the swimming pool. And the two things I remember most were, first, Ali couldn't swim, not a bit; and second, Ali had never thrown a punch underwater in his life—he just made it up. . . . but it got him in *Life*. . . . Now that's genius you don't see in people very often. Genius, and a bit of a con man, too.

Clay couldn't swim when he demonstrated how to box underwater.

CASSIUS CLAY, POET

Clay's growing use of hyperbole to hasten his fame is displayed here in this poem from 1964.

"This is the legend of Cassius Clay,
The most beautiful fighter in the world today.
He talks a great deal, and brags indeed-y,
Of a muscular punch that's incredibly speed-y.
The fistic world was dull and weary,
But with a champ like Liston, things had to be dreary.
Then someone with color and someone with dash,
Brought fight fans a runnin' with Cash.
This brash young boxer is something to see,
And the heavyweight championship is his des-tin-y.
This kid fights great; he's got speed and endurance,
But if you sign to fight him, increase your insurance.
This kid's got a left; this kid's got a right,
If he hit you once, you're asleep for the night.
And as you lie on the floor while the ref counts ten,
You'll pray that you won't have to fight me again.

For I am the man this poem's about,
The next champ of the world, there isn't a doubt.
This I predict and I know the score,
I'll be champ of the world in '64.
When I say three, they'll go in the third,
So don't bet against me, I'm a man of my word.
He is the greatest! Yes! I am the man this poem's about,
I'll be champ of the world, there isn't a doubt.
Here I predict Mr. Liston's dismemberment,
I'll hit him so hard; he'll wonder where October
   and November went.
When I say two, there's never a third,
Standin' against me is completely absurd.
When Cassius says a mouse can outrun a horse,
Don't ask how; put your money where your mouse is!
I AM THE GREATEST!"

—1964

CHAPTER TWO

GOING PRO

"The fight is won or lost far away from witnesses—behind the lines, in the gym, and out there on the road, long before I dance under those lights."

The 1962 Clay-Moore bout demonstrated that the student had far outstripped the teacher.

PROFESSIONAL DEBUT

On October 29, 1960, Clay made his professional debut against a police chief from Fayetteville, West Virginia, named Tunney Hunsaker. Although Hunsaker came in sporting a record of seventeen wins against eight defeats, he was clearly one of those overmatched, mostly harmless first-time opponents that many a promising boxing career has started with. Clay dominated the shorter, slower Hunsaker on his way to a six-round decision and first professional win. Hunsaker would later say about Clay, "He was fast as lightning."

Clay's record from his first few years fighting as a pro was almost embarrassingly perfect—19 and 0 with 15 knockouts. Most of his opponents didn't know what had hit them.

CLAY'S FIRST FIGHT AT MADISON SQUARE GARDEN

On March 22, 1960, Cassius Clay made his first official appearance at Madison Square Garden, taking on Gary Jawish in the Inter-City Championships. Even though Jawish had never been knocked down and outweighed Clay by sixty pounds, Clay, according to announcer Jack Smith, "knocked him down for a nine-count with a shattering right in the third."

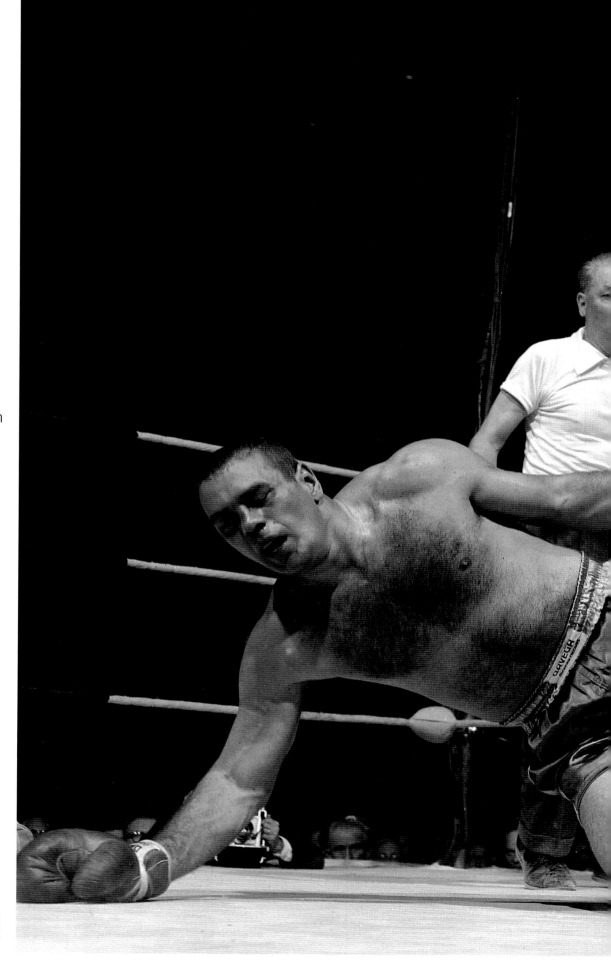

Cassius Clay knocks down
Gary Jawish with a powerful
right hook in the third round.

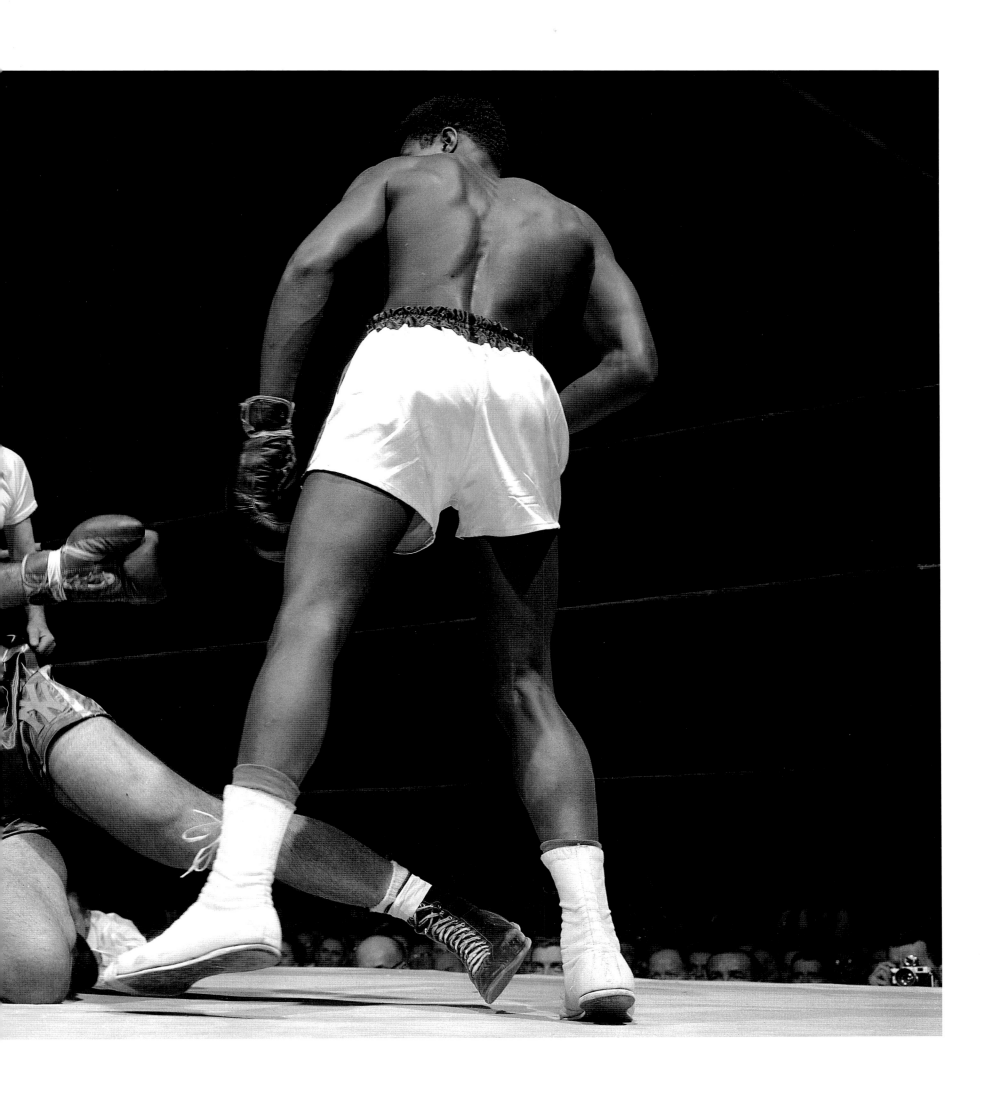

TRAINING WITH ARCHIE MOORE

"To tell you the truth, the boy needed a good spanking, but I wasn't sure who could give it to him."
—ARCHIE MOORE ON CASSIUS CLAY

In November 1960 Cassius Clay went to train with former light heavyweight champion Archie Moore at his facility in Ramona, California. Moore who was forty-seven at the time (and still fighting!) had enough bouts and boxing stories under his belt to fill two careers. The "Old Mongoose" had won his light heavyweight title in 1952 at the age of 39, at the time, the oldest man ever to accomplish that feat. Throughout the 1950s he successfully defended his light heavyweight title while also moving up in weight class and occasionally fighting as a heavyweight. In fact, in 1955 he fought Rocky Marciano for his heavyweight title and even knocked the champ down in the second round, an incredibly rare occurrence. Marciano would go on to win the fight, which would prove to be his final title defense.

Moore persevered and was still recognized by many boxing authorities as the light heavyweight champ when Clay showed up on his doorstep. Although he was mainly focused on his own career, Moore was admittedly anxious to teach the young Olympic champion what he knew. The two men got along well enough, but Clay bristled at some of Moore's training techniques as well as his camp rules, which required all fighters taking on chores such as mopping floors and washing dishes. Their partnership would not be long-lived—Clay went home for Christmas and never came back.

Archie Moore poses beside a picture of the great Rocky Marciano. Moore famously floored Marciano in the second round of their title fight in September 1955.

FIGHTING ARCHIE MOORE

"He will be mine, in round nine, and I ain't lyin'.
He must fall in eight, to prove that I am great.
He wanted to go to heaven, so I took him in seven.
If he'd be in a word of fix, I cut it to six.
If he keeps talkin' jive, he will fall in five.
If he makes me sore, I'll get him in round four, like before,
with Archie Moore, on the floor.
If that don't do, we'll get him in two.
If he runs, we can get him in one.
If he don't wanna fight, he should keep his ugly self at
home that night."

On November 15, 1962, the two men faced off against each other in the ring for real this time. Clay predicted that he would knock out his almost-fifty-year-old opponent in four rounds, while Moore countered that he had come up with a special punch called "The Lip Buttoner," which would finally silence the man whom some had taken to calling "The Louisville Lip." Clay's prediction came true when he knocked Moore out in the fourth.

Moore retired from the ring in 1963 with well over 200 fights and 141 knockouts to his credit. He remained an active trainer of boxers, including future champion George Foreman, and he holds the distinction of being the only man to have fought both Rocky Marciano and Muhammad Ali.

Clay floors the forty-nine-year-old light-heavyweight champion Archie Moore in the fourth round, winning by a technical knockout.

THE MOVE TO MIAMI

"Born in Kentucky, Muhammad Ali was made in Miami."
—TAGLINE FOR PBS DOCUMENTARY *MADE IN MIAMI*

When top fight trainer Angelo Dundee was visiting Louisville in 1957 with light heavyweight Willie Pastrano, Cassius Clay called their hotel room from the lobby phone and asked if he could come up for a few minutes. The two men ended up talking to the local Golden Gloves champ for more than three hours as Clay questioned them about training protocols, especially sparring, road work, and diet.

When Clay returned from Rome with the gold medal, Dundee invited him to train at the 5th Street Gym in Miami, but it wasn't until Clay parted ways with Archie Moore (and after he'd won his first professional fight) that he moved to Miami—and entered a significant new chapter of his life.

Miami was less overtly segregated than Clay's hometown; it was a melting pot of white, black, Hispanic, Creole, and other island ethnicities. Ali found a room at the historic 1896 Charles Hotel in Overtown, the culturally thriving black section of Miami—the Harlem of the South, some called it—and during his running workouts he often crossed the beautiful causeway connecting Miami Beach to Miami proper. This city of blue water, Art Deco buildings, and swaying palms must have felt like a tropical paradise to a kid from gritty, urban Louisville.

The 5th Street Gym soon became a haven for the young fighter. It was "an island of democracy in a world of segregation," according to fight doctor Ferdie Pacheco. Although there were "unwritten" requirements for being accepted to train there—talent, ambition to fight and to win, and the desire to learn from previous champions—Clay was brimming over with all of them. Dundee himself said Clay could "light up" the gym just by walking through the door, a measure of star quality that was not lost on others, and the trainer believed that everyone at 5th Street truly loved him.

Cassius Clay tenderly kisses an adoring fan in Miami, Florida, in February 1964.

AMATEUR VS. PROFESSIONAL

Dundee realized from the start that Clay's boxing technique left a lot to be desired, but he also saw the kid had a lot of skills to compensate for those flaws. The trainer had worked with enough "instinctive" boxers to know that the best way to school them was by offering some subtle coaching and then letting them figure the rest out for themselves. But why was it that Clay, a gold medal Olympian, needed so much tuning up?

The answer lies in the vast difference between amateur boxing and its big, grown-up cousin, professional prizefighting. Unlike a lot of other sports where the amateur basically has to upgrade his or her game to move to the pros, prizefighting requires the athlete to reexamine every aspect of his approach, style, technique, skill, and stamina. After all, if you lose a pro tennis match badly, you probably won't end up in the emergency room. Pro boxers, on the other hand, are putting their physical well-being on the line every time they climb between those ropes.

RULES AND OBJECTIVES

The main differences between the two versions of boxing are in the rules and the objectives.

Amateur rules, naturally, are geared to protect the health of the boxer and are uniform in all AIBA-affiliated countries. Pro boxing has numerous state commissions, all with different sets of rules and guidelines. For instance, mouthpieces are required for all amateur bouts, but in certain states, the pros can fight without them.

The length and quantity of amateur rounds varies between junior and senior and male and female, but the maximum for males is three three-minute rounds, and, for females, four two-minute rounds. Professional fights, on the other hand, run from four up to fifteen three-minute rounds (two-minute rounds for females). Amateurs wear headguards, which are forbidden in pro fights, even though they reduce cuts by 90 percent and earlobe damage by 100 percent. There are twenty-one possible fouls in amateur bouts, many of which are allowed in the pros.

As for objectives, the aim of an amateur fighter is simply to score points for hits, and a knockdown still counts as one hit. In the pros, the harder the hit, the more likely the fighter will disable the opponent and win the round. The knockdown and knockout are intentionally sought.

Also, amateurs compete for the love of the sport and to win for their team or gym and because they have pride in their town, state, or country. They do not box for money, and do not receive payments, bonuses, or commercial endorsements the way the pros do.

OPPOSITE PAGE: Chris Dundee's celebrated 5th Street Gym in Miami Beach, Florida

NEXT PAGE: Clay skipping in the ring during a training session

THE 5TH STREET GYM: "OZ" FOR BOXERS

Fight promoter Chris Dundee—"the Wizard of Oz"—opened the 5th Street Gym in 1950 with the support of his brother, trainer Angelo Dundee—"the Prince of Oz." While the actual piece of real estate was a crumbling building in a failed neighborhood of Miami Beach, the spirit of the place shone like precious metal. Boxing pros the world over were soon sending their young fighters to train there. The gym also drew celebrities up its rickety staircase to watch the hopefuls spar and work the speed bag. Joe Louis, Rocky Marciano, the Beatles, Sean Connery, Frank Sinatra, and Sylvester Stallone, plus a long list of other luminaries, all came to call and stayed to soak up the atmosphere.

Although a host of champions emerged from its doors in addition to Cassius Clay, the gym eventually went into a decline and the building was bulldozed in 2002 to make way for a parking lot. Now all that remains is a plaque.

Recently, however, plans got underway for a revival of the gym at a location one block north. Matt Baiamonte, Angelo's top trainer; conditioner Dino Spencer, who trained under Freddie Roach; and fight promoter Tom Tsatas spearheaded the project. The new gym also received the blessing of Angelo Dundee and his son, Jimmy. The fabled sports Mecca reopened in 2010 and now offers martial arts and cardio workouts in addition to fight training, ensuring the gym a steady stream of customers. Although the old aura may be gone, it's possible the ghosts of the greats still linger in this modern version of that hallowed hall.

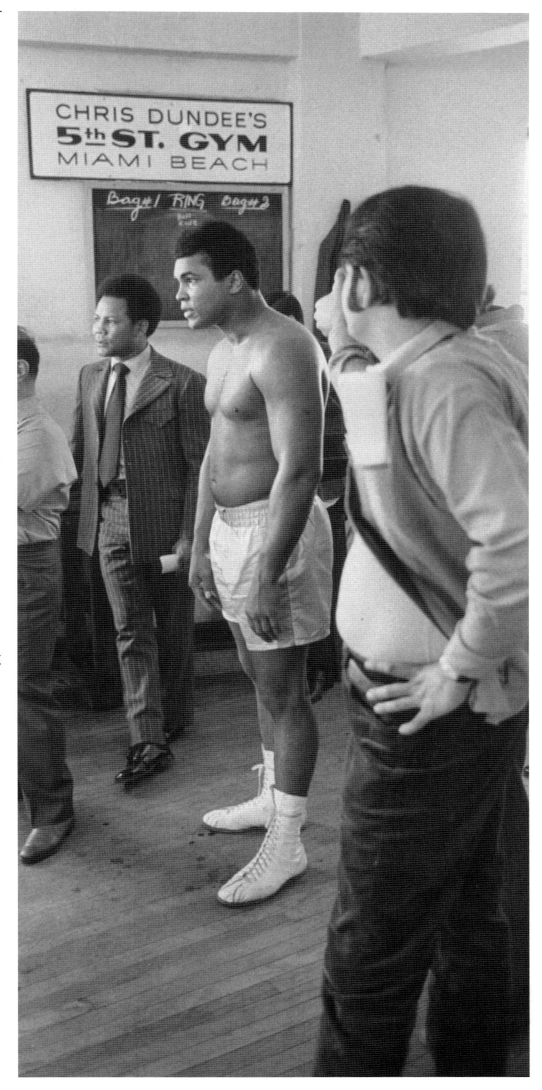

"Float like a butterfly,
sting like a bee;
the hand can't hit
what the eye can't see."

ANGELO DUNDEE

"In private, Muhammad was a quiet person. He was always contemplating something. But in front of people he was a magician. He was the most accessible athlete of his era."

—ANGELO DUNDEE, TRAINER

This Philadelphia native learned his trade during World War II; he worked as a cornerman, mainly at military boxing tournaments in England, while in the Army Air Force. After the war he furthered his education as a boxing trainer and cornerman at Stillman's Gym near the old Madison Square Garden in New York. In the early 1950s he helped brother Chris launch the 5th Street Gym in Miami. Welterweight/middleweight Carmen Basilio became the first champion Angelo handled, seeing him through bouts with Tony DeMarco and Sugar Ray Robinson.

Although he was born Angelo Mirena, he took the name Dundee after his brother Joe fought under as "Johnny Dundee." Their brother Chris also adopted the surname.

Dundee not only guided the young Cassius Clay through his early professional career, he was there in his corner for every fight except two: Tunney Hunsaker in 1960 and Jimmy Ellis in 1971, when Dundee was in Ellis's corner—with Ali's blessing.

Clay was such a natural that Dundee quickly learned that a "hands-off" approach was best.

Instead of instructing him in boxing technique, Dundee strove to make his young protégé believe that any moves he subtly suggested were things Clay had thought of himself.

In the mid-1960s, after Ali hired representatives of the Nation of Islam to manage his career—and Dundee was the only white man on the team—Angelo said he never felt a "black-white divide." He firmly believed that he and Ali "had this special thing, a unique blend, a chemistry.

Dundee trained fifteen world champions over the course of six decades, including Ali, Sugar Ray Leonard, George Foreman, Basilio, and Jose Napoles. He was the perfect cornerman: quick to patch up an embattled fighter, ready with a rallying cry or words of inspiration, and gifted with the ability to shift strategies on the fly in mid-fight. "Angie" was also known for sussing the vulnerabilities of the opposition. Ali recalls, "You come back to the corner and he'll say, 'He's open for a hook.'"

The trainer, who was beloved for the sweetness of his nature, would often say, "It doesn't cost anything more to be nice." There

The legendary boxing trainer Angelo Dundee was renowned for his good nature and supremely positive mentality.

were occasional controversies, however. George Foreman's team accused Dundee of loosening the ropes for Ali before the fight in Zaire, which the trainer always denied. Then again, when the officials at "the Rumble in the Jungle" threatened to tighten the ropes in the middle of the fight, Dundee held up the next round by arguing with them.

Dundee died at the age of ninety, shortly after attending Ali's seventieth birthday party in Louisville. His son said the visit with Ali meant "everything" to his father.

"No matter how bad things were, [Angelo] always put a positive spin on them. That's why Ali loved him so much."
—Bob Arum, CEO and founder of Top Rank (boxing promotions)

THE CORNER TEAM

After making the move to the 5th Street Gym in Miami and taking on Angelo Dundee as his trainer, Cassius Clay found the perfect corner team to keep him primed and fit—two talented, larger-than-life men who remained with him for many years.

DREW BUNDINI BROWN, CORNERMAN AND POET (1928–1987)

This former merchant marine from Midway, Florida, was originally part of Sugar Ray Robinson's entourage. He joined Ali as cornerman and assistant trainer in 1963 and was with him at his final fight in 1981. Brown also helped as a speechwriter for the brash young boxer and wrote the famous rhyme, "Float like a butterfly, sting like a bee, your hands can't hit what your eyes can't see."

Brown was often filmed with Ali before fights, the two of them egging each other on, posturing and chanting for the cameras with their mouths wide open. Ferdie Pacheco said that Brown and Ali had a "mystic connection" and that Brown was almost like the boxer's "guru." True or not, it seemed as though nobody could get the champ pumped up like Bundini.

Brown enjoyed acting occasionally and appeared in a number of hit films, including *Shaft* and *The Color Purple*, as well as several of the Ali documentaries. After marrying Rhoda Palestine, a Caucasian and a Jew, he eventually converted to Reform Judaism. Their son, Drew Jr., became a jet fighter pilot and was, historically, the first black Jew to fly off an aircraft carrier.

Brown died in 1987 in a Los Angeles hospital, just prior to undergoing surgery. He was just fifty-seven years old. He had often spoken of writing an autobiography centered around his life with Ali, but it apparently never came together. In the 1990s, some of his writing did end up on the auction block.

The legendary Drew Bundini Brown: longtime trainer, colorful motivator, ringside cornerman, and part-time poet and actor

FERDIE PACHECO, FIGHT DOCTOR AND PAINTER (B. 1927)

After graduating from medical school, this Tampa native (of Spanish ancestry by way of Cuba) set up a clinic in the Little Havana section of Miami. It wasn't long before he was working with the local boxers at Chris and Angelo Dundee's 5th Street Gym. In 1962, he became the personal physician and cornerman for Cassius Clay and attended the champ until the late 1970s, when Pacheco parted ways with Ali because the fighter ignored his advice to retire. By the time Ferdie permanently gave up his cornerman status to become a TV broadcaster, the "Fight Doctor" had ministered to a total of twelve world champions.

Pacheco spent twenty-five years in this second career, working as a boxing commentator at NBC (he was also their boxing consultant for ten years), Showtime, and Univision, resulting in two Emmy wins. He has also written fourteen books and penned countless newspaper articles and columns.

Pacheco, who displayed a talent for drawing at the age of five, is an internationally recognized artist whose wildly imaginative and boldly colored paintings have been exhibited both in galleries and online, and twice won awards in France.

A documentary film based on his life, *The World of the Fight Doctor*, aired on HBO in 2004.

ALEJANDRO LAVORANTE

"I don't always know what I'm talking about, but I know I'm right!"

Just prior to fighting Archie Moore, Clay went up against the former Argentinian amateur champion on July 20, 1962, at the Los Angeles Sports Arena.

The smoothly handsome Lavorante—once a chauffeur for deposed dictator Juan Peron—had been discovered by Jack Dempsey, who recommended him to American manager Paul "Pinkey" George. After his surprise knockout of top-rated Zora Folley, Lavorante found himself ranked #4 by *The Ring* magazine. In 1961 a California promoter offered World Heavyweight Champion Floyd Patterson half a million dollars to battle Lavorante. Patterson held out for a million, so the fight never materialized.

Once in the ring with Lavorante, Clay appeared rocky at first. Then he took control in the third round, displaying, as the announcer described it, "the movement, footwork, quick hands, and boxing skill he was renowned for." As the fight progressed, the crowd in the arena watched Clay score repeatedly with jabs, straight punches, and swift combinations, until Lavorante ran out of gas.

Clay had predicted, "Lavorante will fall in five," which he did, the result of a knockout.

Sadly, in his very next fight, against John Riggins in Los Angeles, the young South American fighter sustained severe injuries while being knocked out and lapsed into a coma. His father returned with him to Argentina, where he died nineteen months after the fateful bout. Critics of ring violence pointed out that the boxer had been knocked out in all three of his most recent fights, including a loss to Archie Moore, where he'd been carried out on a stretcher.

Clay blocks Lavorante's left hook and counters with a powerful left hook of his own.

CHARLIE POWELL

"It's hard to be humble when you're as great as I am."

Texan Charlie Powell, powerful and athletic since boyhood, played Class B baseball for the St. Louis Browns for one season before he was drafted by the NFL. At nineteen, he was the youngest football player in the organization's history. Powell spent five seasons with the San Francisco 49ers and two with the Oakland Raiders.

He also boxed professionally and, in 1959, knocked out Cuban Nino Valdes, the second-ranked heavyweight in the world.

Clay met Powell in Pittsburgh on January 24, 1963, and predicted that he would "annihilate" him in the third round. When Powell was knocked out in the third round by a hard right followed by a left hook, Clay pronounced himself the "prophet of the fight game." Unfortunately, the truncated fight drew boos from the crowd.

Powell said he fought the wrong type of fight. "I stood still and tried to floor him with one punch. I should have jabbed more and kept the pressure on him." Clay responded by admitting that Powell hurt him in the second round with a left hook. "It shook me," Clay confessed. Powell had also turned the tables on Clay, taunting him during the first two rounds, saying, "Come on, big mouth. It's nearly round three." But Clay kept his cool and waited until he saw the fear in Powell's eyes during the third round. "Kill the head and you die," Clay declared. He acknowledged that Powell was the roughest competitor he had met yet, at least "for three rounds."

Powell later went up against another future heavyweight champion, Floyd Patterson, who defeated him in six rounds.

Clay fulfils his prediction of defeating Powell in the third round of their contest at the Civic Arena, Pittsburgh, Pennsylvania.

DOUG JONES
"THE FIGHT OF THE YEAR"

"People say I missed my prediction, 'cause the fight went ten rounds. First I said Jones in four, then I said Jones in six. Six and four is what?"

In March 1963, Clay squared off against another heavyweight contender, Doug Jones, in New York City's Madison Square Garden. As had become his trademark, Clay dismissed Jones as a bum and started firing off predictions as to which round he would knock him out. He started by saying that he would floor Jones in six but later adjusted it in his usual rhyming fashion to: "I'm changing the pick I made before. Instead of six, Doug goes in four." This time, however, it didn't exactly go as planned.

Jones came out and challenged Clay from the opening bell. When the fourth round passed and Clay failed to achieve his predicted knockout, the crowd grew disenchanted. In the end, the fight went the full ten rounds, with Clay winning a unanimous decision. The two ringside judges had him winning by the narrowest of margins while the referee (acting as third judge) had him winning eight rounds to one, with one a draw. Whether this lackluster outcome would remove some of the smugness and light a fire under Clay remained to be seen.

Jones catches Clay straight in the mouth in the first round of the fight that the boxing magazine *The Ring* hailed as "the fight of the year" in 1963.

HENRY COOPER

"Henry Cooper is nothing to me, if that bum goes over the fifth round I won't return to the United States for 30 days, and that's final."

LEFT: With seconds remaining at the end of the round four, Cooper unleashes a vicious left hook, "Enry's 'Ammer." The astonished Clay falls backward onto the ropes.

NEXT PAGE: Clay gives an assist to Ingemar Johansson. Clay served as Johansson's sparring partner before the heavyweight challenger's 1961 title fight with Floyd Patterson

Coming off his disappointing effort versus Doug Jones in New York, Clay took his act to London to face British champ Henry Cooper, known for his powerful left hook—or "'Enry's 'Ammer." As usual, Clay made a prediction prior to the fight; Cooper would fall in five. Cooper was eight years Ali's senior and a seasoned fighter, but that would do little to help him make up for his American opponent's size and speed advantage.

A crowd of 55,000 fans packed London's Wembley Stadium to support their countryman. But for the first three rounds of the fight, they found little to cheer about, as Clay hit Cooper at will. In the fourth Clay just seemed to be toying with his bloodied opponent when Cooper landed a wild left hook that sent Clay flying into the ropes and onto the seat of his trunks in the round's waning seconds. He got to his feet, clearly dazed, as the bell sounded.

Luckily for Clay, he had a split in one of his gloves, a mishap that trainer Angelo Dundee exploited, pointing it out to the referee in an effort to buy his man some time. Although there was nothing they could do to fix the glove, the ploy worked. Clay was able to clear the cobwebs from his brain and absolutely tore Cooper apart in round five until the ref stopped it. Clay had dodged a bullet and next hoped to take aim at Sonny Liston's heavyweight title.

CHAPTER THREE

THE HEAVY-WEIGHT TITLE

"There are no pleasures in a fight but some of my fights have been a pleasure to win."

Cassius Clay and his team are exultant upon winning the heavyweight crown in the battle that *The Ring* magazine hailed as the "Fight of the Decade."

SONNY LISTON

"I remember thinking that a dark cloud would fall over young Cassius Clay the night he fought the brutal Sonny Liston."

—DAVID HALBERSTAM, AUTHOR

After defeating Cooper, Clay's ranking improved, but he was still not the number-one or two contender for the crown (reports vary from third to ninth in rank). Yet he began targeting Sonny Liston, the current heavyweight champ, as his next opponent. He bragged and boasted, he teased and taunted, trying to lure Liston's management into agreeing to a fight.

Eventually a match was scheduled for February 25, 1964, at Miami's Convention Hall, but when rumors of Clay's association with Malcolm X, a member of the controversial Nation of Islam (or Black Muslims) surfaced, fight promoter Bill Faversham threatened to cancel the bout. He feared, it was said, if the news got out that Clay had Black Muslim sympathies white fans would stay away and "kill the gate." As a compromise, Clay agreed not to discuss his new allegiance until after the fight. As it was, the arena was barely half full on the day of the event.

A FORMIDABLE FOE

The man who stood between Cassius Clay and the world heavyweight title was a formidable boxer who brought frightening power to his punches. He was mob-connected and therefore not someone to be taken lightly, not a man who tolerated—or possibly even understood—Clay's baiting and foolish wordplay.

Charles L. "Sonny" Liston grew up on a sharecropper's farm in St. Francis County, Arkansas, one of thirteen children. He didn't even know the exact year of his birth, because it was unlikely it had ever been registered. As a child, he suffered such fierce whippings from his father that they left lifelong scars. Like many poor boys before him, he was drawn into gang crime and became known as the Yellow Shirt Bandit. Yet after being arrested in 1950 and sent to the Missouri State Penitentiary for committing a violent robbery, Liston's life began to turn around. The prison's athletic director, Father Alois Stevens, harnessed the young man's anger and strength in the confines of a boxing ring— and aided him in getting an early parole.

Sonny Liston takes a break from training. Clay goaded Liston mercilessly before their fight, insisting that Liston was "too ugly to be the world's champ."

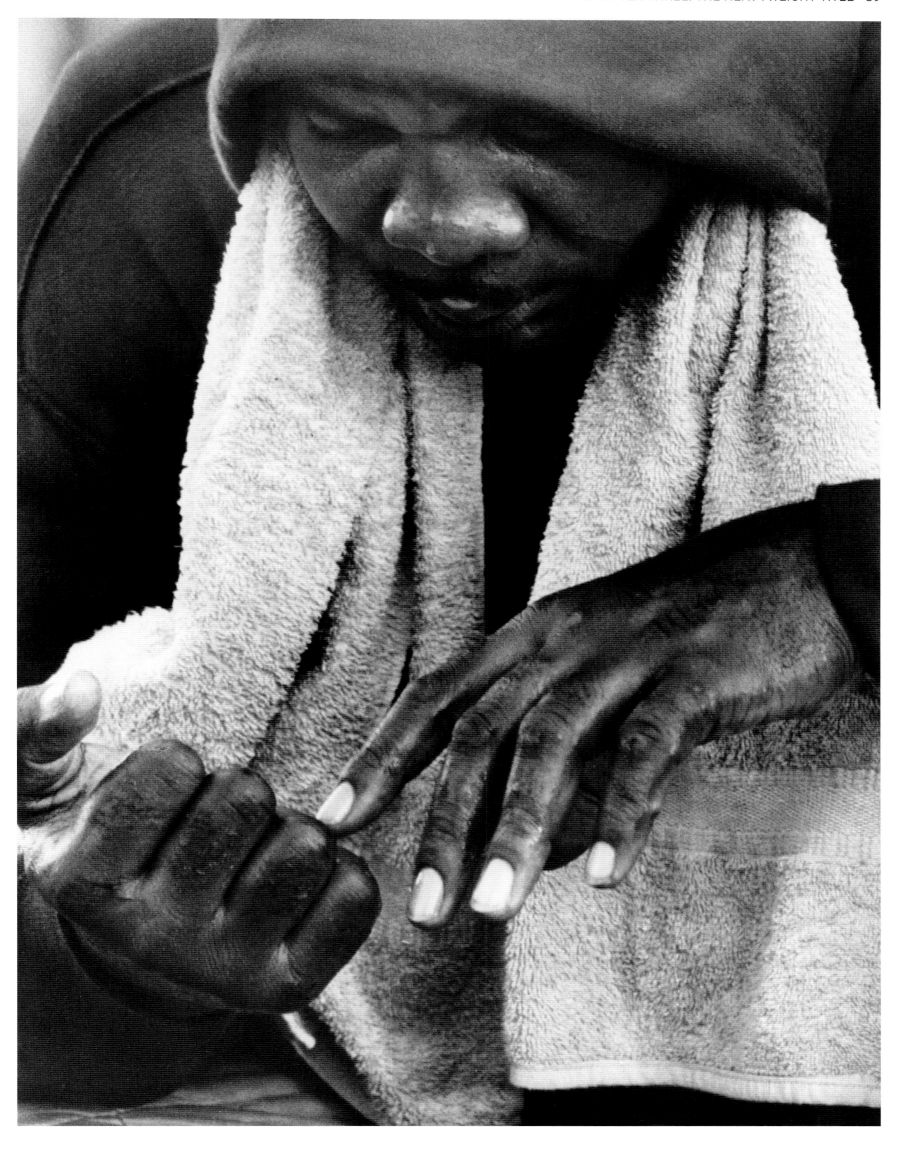

Liston quickly won several amateur boxing tournaments on the outside, including the Golden Gloves, and word began to spread of this fearsome fighter. When he knocked out European bronze medalist Hermann Schreibauer barely two minutes into the first round, St. Louis Golden Gloves coach Tony Anderson labeled Liston the strongest fighter he had ever seen.

Called "Big Bear," the six-foot, one-half-inch Liston earned the nickname not for his height, but rather for his immense power and an unusually long reach, especially with his left arm. On September 2, 1953, Liston debuted professionally in St. Louis with a first-round knockout of Don Smith. Throughout the 1950s, he battled his way up through the ranks until 1962, when he bested champion Floyd Patterson with a shocking first-round knockout to gain the heavyweight title.

DOUBTERS ON THE SIDELINES

Based on the vulnerability Clay had shown to Henry Cooper's left hook, sports journalists and boxing touts predicted the twenty-two-year-old challenger would quickly fall to Liston's fearsome left fist. Jim Murray of the *Los Angeles Times* quipped, "The only thing at which Clay can beat Liston is reading the dictionary." Joe Nichols of the *New York Times* refused to even attend, convinced it would be a pitiful mismatch. On the day of the bout, Clay was a seven-to-one shot, and forty-three out of forty-six onsite sportswriters picked Liston to win by a knockout.

Sonny Liston became World Heavyweight Champion in 1962 by knocking out Floyd Patterson in the first round. His first title defense was a rematch in which Patterson lasted four seconds longer than he did the first time around.

CLAY TAUNTS LISTON

"Sonny Liston is nothing. The man can't talk. The man can't fight. The man needs talking lessons. The man needs boxing lessons. And since he's gonna fight me, he needs falling lessons."

To those who followed boxing, Sonny Liston seemed almost invincible. Many sportswriters and fight fans, unable to envision a contender who could take down this juggernaut, predicted his reign would last indefinitely. Even Clay acknowledged that when Liston punched your arm, he just about broke it. So Clay decided he needed to give himself a psychological edge over the champ.

He began a campaign to demoralize Liston with a series of pranks, using bullhorns to accost him, chasing his car with a bear collar and leash while spouting insults, and continuing to batter Sonny with verbal assaults whenever he was near a microphone. Clay even sported a warm-up jacket that said "Bear Huntin'" on the back.

There are plenty who believe Clay's wild tactics hit home, and it's possible they worked precisely because ex-con Liston had learned in prison that it was never prudent to tangle with the crazy inmates. Liston began to appear more and more uneasy, and clearly had few ways to cope mentally with this relentless gadfly.

Clay taunts Liston at the weigh-in before the fight.

"Clay comes out to meet Liston and Liston starts to retreat,
If Liston goes back an inch farther he'll end up in a ringside seat.
Clay swings with a left, Clay swings with a right,
Just look at young Cassius carry the fight.
Liston keeps backing but there's not enough room,
It's a matter of time until Clay lowers the boom.
Then Clay lands with a right, what a beautiful swing,
And the punch raised the bear clear out of the ring.
Liston still rising and the ref wears a frown,
But he can't start counting until Sonny comes down.
Now Liston disappears from view, the crowd is getting frantic
But our radar stations have picked him up somewhere
   over the Atlantic.
Who on Earth thought, when they came to the fight,
That they would witness the launching of a human satellite.
Hence the crowd did not dream, when they laid down
   their money,
That they would see a total eclipse of Sonny."
                    —CASSIUS CLAY, AS READ ON CBS's I'VE GOT A SECRET

CLAY'S UNIQUE STYLE

"I got the height, the reach, the weight, the physique, the speed, the courage, the stamina, and the natural ability that's going to make me great. Putting it another way, to beat me you got to be greater than great."

Dundee saw almost immediately that his new protégé did a number of things wrong when it came to technique, including telegraphing his right uppercut by dropping his right hand. Furthermore, Clay's customary lowered guard, with his gloves held down near his waist, offered opponents a clean shot at his exposed chin. But Dundee also saw that Clay's amazing reflexes allowed him to feint back, away from any blows. Even then a fighter was vulnerable—when he feinted back he was off balance, making him easier to knock down. But Clay just danced away from any threat. His speed, agility, and ability to take a hit compensated for his technical flaws, and so Angelo allowed him to box "his way." As Frazier/Norton/Holmes trainer, Eddie Futch, saw it, "Ali takes his mistakes, shows them to you, and then beats you with them."

Naturally, this unorthodox boxing style initially earned the young fighter a lot of flak from sportswriters, so Angelo bolstered Clay's hurt feelings by telling him his style made him unique among fighters. It wasn't long before Clay believed him . . . and that burgeoning ego began to stir.

Clay showing his moves to a roomful of reporters.

"I'm so fast that last night I turned off the light switch in my hotel room and was in bed before the room was dark."

FANCY FOOTWORK

Whenever he watched footage of past fights, Clay focused on the great champs—Jack Dempsey, Joe Louis, Rocky Marciano—but these viewings always left him puzzled. Where was their footwork? Where were their evasive tactics? "They just stand there flat-footed and throw punches," he complained, recalling how Fred Stoner had made a point of teaching him to dance gracefully around the ring.

Eventually Clay would find a kindred spirit in welterweight/middleweight champion Sugar Ray Robinson, who, like Clay, was famed for his dazzling footwork, fluid movement, and fast jabs. The Associated Press voted Robinson the best boxer of the twentieth century and ESPN named him the greatest fighter in history—assessments that Clay, a future "greatest," came to share. At last Clay had footage to study that reflected his own style in the ring.

THE DOUBLE-CLUTCH SHUFFLE

Another fighter Clay emulated was the great heavyweight Jersey Joe Walcott. Angelo Dundee acknowledged that Clay adapted much of his style from Walcott, including a move on which the boxer would rapidly slide alternate feet back and forth. It came to be called the Ali Shuffle or the double-clutch shuffle, and the boxer—a talented amateur magician—used it to create a classic misdirection, drawing his opponent's eyes down to the mat. The fighter also did the shuffle to show he was confidently in control of a match or to signal just before an opponent hit the canvas. It sometimes appeared that he was letting his feet do the bragging.

Dundee admits that Walcott used the move first. "Walcott invented it," he said, "while Ali popularized it." Dundee also pointed out that Ali usually built up a lot of nervous energy during a fight, and the shuffle acted as a safety valve to help him release those jitters and regain his rhythm.

Clay joking with his idol, Sugar Ray Robinson.

MEET THE BEATLES

On February 18, 1964, just seven days before the title bout, the Liverpool singing sensations, the Beatles, were invited to visit Cassius Clay at his Miami training camp in the 5th Street Gym. Clay cheerfully mugged and posed with the Fab Four, who gamely played victim for the charismatic young fighter in a series of photos.

George Harrison recalled, "It was a big publicity thing. It was all part of being a Beatle . . . getting lugged around and then thrust into rooms full of press men taking pictures and asking questions. Muhammad Ali was quite cute."

Before Clay entered the gym, John Lennon wondered aloud why they weren't visiting the camp of title-holder Sonny Liston, whom everyone expected to win the upcoming fight. But when Clay finally joined them, John seemed quite amused by his antics. Drummer Ringo Starr added his own reminiscence, "I sparred with Cassius Clay—as he was then known. I taught him everything he knew."

Paul, John, Ringo, and George take a hit from the Greatest.

THE FIGHT

On the morning of the fight, Clay continued to badger Liston, turning the usually businesslike weighing-in ceremony into a media circus, hurling insults and lunging at the champ. He and Drew Bundini Brown posed together and recited in unison, "Float like a butterfly, sting like a bee." Liston, remote and somber, continued to eye his challenger warily. Many onlookers believed Clay's frenzied behavior was a sign of his uncontrolled panic and feared for the cocky young fighter.

Once the combatants entered the ring, everyone at ringside was impressed with Liston's manner, calm and sure, as befit a champion. He also looked decidedly ominous, a human "Godzilla" in his hooded robe. The members of the audience held their breath as the two men stepped forward to touch gloves, and then they gasped. Clay, at six foot three, was inches taller than Liston, towering above him, forcing the champ to look up to meet his eyes. Clay had scored yet another point in the psychological battle.

Liston catches Clay with
a stinging left jab.

"If Sonny Liston whups me I'll kiss his feet in the ring, I'll crawl out of the ring on my knees, I'll tell him he is the greatest and get the first jet to get out of the country."

Clay's speed stymied Liston almost from the first bell. The champ seemed baffled by Clay's rapid footwork and lightning jabs. Liston's energy appeared to evaporate during those early rounds, leaving him flat-footed and leaden.

Then, after the third round, Liston's cornerman "juiced" or "burned" his gloves, smearing astringent on them, intending the substance to rub off into Clay's eyes and irritate them. When the bout resumed, the announcer quickly saw that Clay was in trouble, fighting blind and repeatedly blinking his eyes. When the round ended, a disoriented Clay wanted Dundee to cut off his gloves and admit defeat, but the trainer refused, reminding Clay that this fight was for the world heavyweight title. Dundee cleansed his eyes the best he could and sent his fighter back for a fifth round, telling him to "run" until

his vision cleared. By the sixth round Clay could see better, and he began to pummel Liston in retaliation for the foul, ending the round by landing two punishing left hooks

Back in his corner after the bell, Liston spit out his mouthpiece and muttered, "That's it." Yet his crew kept working, applying Vaseline to his face. When they refit his mouthpiece, he spit it out again. "I said that's it."

The champ had refused to return to the fight, and as Clay danced impatiently at the center of the ring awaiting the inevitable decision, a clamor arose from the crowd, some shouting with wild joy at witnessing such an upset, others insisting the bout had been fixed. And why shouldn't they complain? It was virtually unheard of for a world champion to withdraw so stonily; they usually went down fighting, in a flurry of fists and blood.

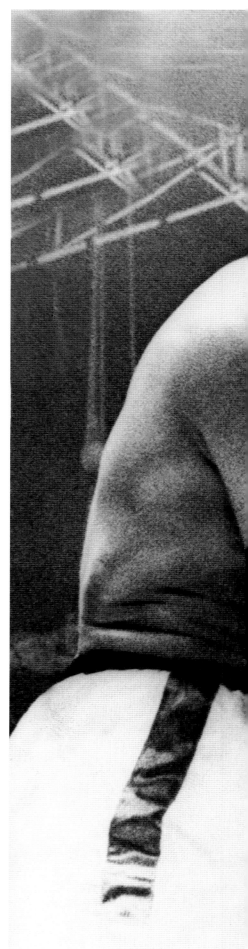

Clay attempts to get Liston into a clinch.

"I'm king of the world! I'm pretty! I'm a bad man! I shook up the world!"

Clay, recalling those final rounds, said, "I hit him with eight punches in a row until he doubled up. I remember thinking something like, 'Yeah, you old sucker! You try to be all big and bad!' He was gone. He knew he couldn't last. . . . I missed with a right that would have dropped him. But I jabbed and jabbed at that cut under his eye, until it was wide open and bleeding worse than before. I knew he wasn't due to last much longer."

Liston's camp made excuses: Sonny had injured his shoulder during training earlier that week. They'd decided to go ahead with the fight in spite of it, they said, believing Clay was no real threat. Someone added that Liston then aggravated the injury throwing a missed punch in the first round.

As for the rumors that the mob had fixed the fight and then bet on long-shot Clay to make a profit, and the protests that there was no way Clay could have won legitimately, Angelo Dundee had an answer: "My guy would have beat Liston every day of the week . . . and twice on Sunday."

"I shook the world!" Clay decreed, and the world agreed. Boxing had an adored new golden boy . . . at least for a few days.

Clay races across the ring in his famously jubilant victory celebration.

CASSIUS CLAY: MEDIA DARLING

"Wait a minute! Sonny Liston is not coming out! The winner and new heavyweight champion of the world is Cassius Clay."
—HOWARD COSELL, BROADCASTING AT RINGSIDE

As a returning Olympic champion, Clay naturally garnered attention from the American press. Once he started to win fights professionally, his fame spread and more interviews were forthcoming. And, of course, once he began to exercise the "Louisville Lip," the news media followed him devoutly. Clay was savvy enough to understand that if he continued to supply them with outrageous boasts, amusing poems, or quotable sounds bites, he would remain a sports reporter's dream.

Just like his role model, wrestler Gorgeous George, Clay didn't mind if some people disliked him, as long as they paid to see him fight. And he could overlook the fact that the media used him, as long as they kept him in the spotlight. In time, Clay morphed into Black Muslim Muhammad Ali, and became more loathed than liked, at least in the beginning. But during his early pro days, he basked in all the press attention, keeping himself in the headlines and his name and antics on the lips of everyone, even those who had never even seen a prizefight.

And the press corps in turn, at least the more astute of its members, somehow sensed that this arrogant, mouthy young boxer would be a world changer, though even they couldn't know that he would become the first black athlete to take his place in history without constraint, without "humbly holding his hat in his hand" to appease the egos and soothe the racial fears of the white audience—as Joe Louis and Jackie Robinson had done to some extent. No, Cassius Clay, soon to become Muhammad Ali, did not see fame as a privilege handed to him by the power base, he saw it as his by right of conquest. And whether the public loved him or hated him during his various controversies, the press never abandoned him. And because of that, the legend, and the hype that surrounded it, only continued to grow.

The "Louisville Lip" lets his right fist do the talking. Some argue that Clay's mouth had been his greatest weapon in his victory over Sonny Liston.

"Eat your words!
Eat your words!
I am the greatest."
—CASSIUS CLAY SHOUTING AT
REPORTERS WHO HAD DISMISSED
HIM AS A BIGMOUTH AND A FRAUD
PRIOR TO HIS FIGHT WITH LISTON.

Clay proclaims his greatness
after defeating Liston.

CHAPTER FOUR

A NEW FAITH, A NEW NAME

"Cassius Clay is a slave name. I didn't choose it, and I didn't want it. I am Muhammad Ali, a free name— it means 'beloved of God'—and I insist people use it when speaking to me and of me."

Ali posing with the heavyweight belt before a sign that reads "Allah is the Greatest."

FINDING ANSWERS IN THE NATION OF ISLAM

"Black is beautiful."

—SLOGAN OF THE PRO-BLACK CULTURAL MOVEMENT OF THE 1960s

As Cassius Clay began to mature and learned more about the world outside the boxing ring, his need for spiritual enrichment also increased. Sadly, the Baptist faith of his mother was no longer fulfilling those needs. As a child of segregation, Clay knew firsthand how white people's laws could thwart and diminish black people, and yet old-school Christianity seemed to hold out no immediate answers for a black man who had felt the harsh sting of prejudice. In the teachings and doctrines of the Nation of Islam, however, Clay believed he had found answers to many of his questions, including how a black individual could become proud of his or her heritage and no longer feel inferior or second-rate. He began to attend meetings and talk with the movement's leaders.

So it transpired that in early 1964, even before the bout with Liston, Clay was seen consorting with members of the Nation of Islam (also known as the Black Muslims). And in spite of promoter Bill Faversham's efforts to stamp out rumors of Clay's connection to what was considered a militant group, it is likely a number of disapproving boxing fans learned of his new associates and purposely stayed away from the Liston fight. This was just the beginning of the extreme fan polarity Clay's actions would provoke for years to come.

The morning after the fight, Clay, with the prominent Black Muslim Malcolm X at his side, announced to a basically white press corps that he was, indeed, affiliated with the Nation of Islam. When the press accosted him and Malcolm X while the two ate lunch together, Malcolm X, who never missed a chance to be "on message," declared, "Clay is the finest Negro I have ever known, the man that will mean more to his people than any athlete before him. He is more than Jackie Robinson was, because Robinson was a white man's hero."

The boxer originally announced he was taking the name Cassius X, the X replacing his former "slavemaster" name. But during a March 6 radio broadcast, Nation of Islam leader Elijah Muhammad honored Clay with the name Muhammad Ali (Muhammad meaning "worthy of praise" and Ali for the devout cousin of the Prophet). This new name indicated the fighter was now highly situated in the Muslim echelon, an elevation that took place almost at the same moment that Malcolm X—who himself had hoped to receive such a blessed name—began his fall from grace.

Ali speaking with Malcolm X at a soda-fountain counter as amused fans look on.

ELIJAH MUHAMMAD

"Elijah Muhammad had given me my name, Muhammad Ali. I felt that he had set me free!"

Elijah Muhammad was born Elijah Robert Poole in Georgia, the son of a sharecropper and Baptist lay preacher. The boy barely finished fourth grade before hiring himself out for factory work. As an adult in 1931, he attended a speech given by Wallace Fard Muhammad on the empowering aspects of Islam for people of color. Fard had founded an Islamic movement only a year before in Detroit and he considered himself both the Islamic Mahdi and the Judaic Messiah. Elijah—who had no love for whites, having seen three black men lynched as a youth—was soon a devoted follower of Fard and eventually became his assistant minister in the newly named Nation of Islam (NOI). After Fard's disappearance in 1934, Elijah Muhammad became the group's leader. A conflict with the Detroit chapter led Muhammad to establish a new headquarters in Chicago at Temple No. 2, Mosque Maryam (today presided over by Louis Farrakhan). Later he would establish temples in Milwaukee and Washington, D.C.

The Nation of Islam focused on improving the spiritual and economic situation of African Americans and supported the creation of a separate "black nation." Its teachings required the worship of Allah and promoted the belief that blacks were His chosen people. At the outbreak of World War II, Elijah Muhammad added a new tenet, admonishing his followers not to enlist in the military or report to their draft boards.

Elijah Muhammad addresses the crowd at the Nation of Islam rally in Harlem, New York, on June 28, 1964.

He maintained that America did nothing for black people and that they owed the country no allegiance. He was convicted of violating the Selective Service Act and was jailed for the duration of the war.

The ranks of Black Muslims grew after the war, and around this time a petty criminal named Malcolm Little converted to the faith while still in prison. Malcolm X, as he would call himself, would eventually become Elijah Muhammad's second in command.

In the early 1960s, a famous young boxer named Cassius Clay was showing interest in the NOI. Elijah Muhammad—along with his trusted lieutenant Malcolm X—wooed him to the cause and, after he had won the world heavyweight championship, presented him with a righteous new name, Muhammad Ali. But then Malcolm X grew disenchanted with the leader of the NOI. After accusing Elijah Muhammad of, among other things, fathering children by several of his secretaries, Malcolm X broke with the group, hoping to take Ali with him. But Elijah Muhammad kept Ali close during that time, even sending his son Herbert to travel with the boxer to Africa.

Elijah Muhammad had eight children by his wife, but when he died, nineteen children petitioned the Nation of Islam for support as his heirs. Their claims were refused.

MALCOLM X

"Turning my back on Malcolm was one of the mistakes that I regret most in my life."

The foremost preacher in the Nation of Islam, this charismatic speaker began life as Malcolm Little in Omaha, Nebraska, the son of a Baptist lay minister. His father spoke out against white oppression and made sure his children were proud of their African American heritage. Unfortunately, his children also learned about the deep hatred some whites had for their people—when Malcolm was six his father was killed by a streetcar, most likely pushed by the white supremacists who had repeatedly threatened him, and at least one of his father's brothers was lynched.

Malcolm excelled in school and showed great promise but left in his teens to pursue a life of petty crime. It was while he was serving a prison sentence for burglary that he learned of the Nation of Islam from his brother, a recent convert. The concept of African American self-reliance and the eventual reunification of all African American people, as preached by the NOI, appealed to him, and he began to correspond with Elijah Muhammad. By 1950 he was signing his name Malcolm X, leaving behind Little, which he considered his "slavemaster" name.

Over the next decade Malcolm X was the outspoken voice of the Nation of Islam and did little to endear himself to the U.S. government, protesting the Korean War to President Truman, declaring himself a communist, indicting America for its treatment of minorities, and agitating his listeners by advocating African American supremacy. Meanwhile, as a shrewd and compelling minister, he continued to expand the ranks of the Nation of Islam. In 1957, he gained national exposure for protesting the arrest

and brutal beating of Black Muslim Johnson Hinton, who had tried to stop two New York City policemen from beating a fellow African American.

In 1964, Malcolm X began to appear in photos with Cassius Clay and, by the time of Clay's title match with Sonny Liston, the young fighter had already converted to NOI. Associates of Clay, now called Muhammad Ali, said Malcolm X was a combination big brother and mentor to the boxer, and the two seemed to have forged a deep friendship. But when Malcolm X severed his ties with NOI and founded Muslim Mosque, Inc., Ali turned away from him, no doubt acting on orders from Elijah Muhammad.

Assassins' bullets took the life of Malcolm X on February 21, 1965, as he was about to address the Organization of African American Unity at the Audubon Ballroom in New York City. After a disturbance erupted in the audience, a man rushed toward him, blasting a sawed-off shotgun, while two other men ran onto the stage firing semiautomatic handguns. Malcolm X received twenty-one wounds and was pronounced dead at Columbia Presbyterian Hospital. In an awkward sound bite after the killing, Muhammad Ali stated that, "Malcolm X or anyone who attacks or talks about attacking Elijah Muhammad will die. No man can oppose the messenger of God verbally or physically and get away with it."

Years later, Ali was known to keep a picture taken of him with Malcolm X as a sort of talisman. It was clear to his confidants that he deeply regretted abandoning his friend and mentor.

Malcolm X looks on as Ali signs autographs for admirers in March 1964.

SHOCK AND DISBELIEF: ALI AND THE PRESS

"I believe in the religion of Islam.
I believe in Allah and peace."

When Ali announced that he was indeed a member of the Black Muslims, it sent a shockwave through the media, and subsequently through the country. Nothing like it had ever occurred before; it was unheard of for a young (African American) sports star to oppose (white) authority and ally himself with such a despised and controversial movement. It was downright . . . "uppity."

Furthermore, it seemed to the many people who had enjoyed the fighter's boyish charm, his teasing humor, and his clean-cut good looks, Ali's decision was openly repudiating both America and Christianity. This decision would surely be the death of his career, sportswriters intoned. But then again, some people reasoned, this was the 1960s, America's decade of great change, and perhaps Ali's decision was simply a part of that youthful movement away from hidebound values.

Whether people were for him (at first it seemed as if few were) or against him, Muhammad Ali continued to be a major topic of conversation on TV sports programs, radio call-in shows, and in homes across the country. Young people were even drawn into the dialogue. Ali's initial questioning of authority and the power base was the first inkling anyone had that the young boxer from Louisville would become one of the century's most outspoken and visible proponents of change, not only for blacks but for people of all colors and beliefs. Even Nelson Mandela, locked in his prison cell, was watching Ali's fights and following with great interest the evolution of the young man from pugnacious pugilist to plainspoken public conscience.

Ali cheers at a
Muslim rally in 1965.

DISCOVERING HIS ROOTS IN GHANA

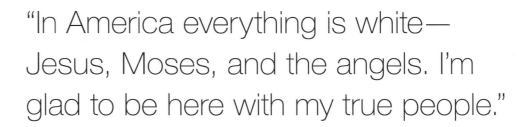

"In America everything is white—Jesus, Moses, and the angels. I'm glad to be here with my true people."

Shortly after the Liston fight and the announcement of his conversion to Islam, Ali decided to make a pilgrimage to Africa to discover his roots. (Malcolm X originally suggested the visit, but Ali had split with his friend before the trip.) So, in May 1964, he traveled to Ghana and met with President Kwame Nkrumah, an anticolonialist, whom Ali declared "a great guy."

Fans, especially children, mobbed the fighter wherever he went. When he called out, "Who's the king?" the crowd would shout back, "You!" It was possibly the first time he got a sense of being an internationally recognized sports hero or of being a role model to other young blacks.

With apparent gusto he sampled local food, cheered up patients in hospitals, visited remote villages, and posed for photographs with the president wearing native Ashanti garb made of kente cloth or—as *Sports Illustrated* described him: "looking like a slice of Old Testament ham . . . in a décolleté shower curtain." But, journalistic levity aside, Ali was earnestly trying to tap into some part of his past beyond that white abolitionist ancestor from the nineteenth century.

He also had another mission . . . to promote his Muslim faith. And to make sure he stayed "on script," Elijah Muhammad's son Herbert accompanied him on the trip.

When it was finally time for Ali to fly home, so many people showed up at the airport there was nearly a riot. "I know one thing," said a local fan with a wide grin, "they never turned out like this for Queen Elizabeth."

Ali greets fans in Ghana.

LISTON REMATCH

"Get up and fight, you bum!
You're supposed to be so bad!
Nobody will believe this!"

In August 1964, Ali wed cocktail waitress and sometime-model Sonji Roi after a month-long courtship. There wasn't much time for a honeymoon, however—the champ had to get into shape for his next fight, a rematch with Sonny Liston scheduled for November at the Boston Garden.

If it were possible, Ali's second fight against now-challenger Liston was even more controversial than the first. In June, the World Boxing Association (WBA) stripped Ali of his title for agreeing to an immediate rematch with Liston, which was against their rules. Just before the fight, however, Ali suffered a hernia and needed emergency surgery. Meanwhile, the fight was said to be "illegal" by some Bay State officials, who claimed the license was not proper. The match ended up being pushed ahead six months to May 25, 1965, with a new venue—a converted high-school hockey rink—in Lewiston, Maine, a town of just 30,000 with an arena that seated only 2,400. But that didn't matter, because there was a deal in place to broadcast the fight to theaters nationwide using closed-circuit TV.

This postponement might have been a fateful postponement for Ali's camp, since Liston was reportedly in tip-top shape in the fall but slacked off training over the winter. Still, Liston came to the rematch as the crowd favorite once again; many fans believed his loss in the first fight was a fluke. Plus, there was now an unspoken sentiment among African American and whites both that Liston was a "decent black man," one who toed the line, unlike Ali who had branded himself as a militant African American. Ironically, "Godzilla" was now the "Good Negro." (It helps to bear in mind that in few sports do allegiances shift as rapidly as in boxing.)

Just before the first bell, Ali prayed in his corner for a moment and then came out swinging, landing a one-two punch to Liston's gut. Angelo Dundee later explained that this was their game plan, "to hit him with a couple of good shots early on, to make him remember the other fight." Liston clearly didn't need much of a reminder: at 1:40 of the first round, Ali responded to a Liston jab with a short downward punch. Most reporters and photographers missed it. But, by then, Liston was flat out on the mat . . . where he stayed after an aborted attempt to rise.

Ali did not go back to a neutral corner, but stood over Liston jeering, "Get up and fight, you

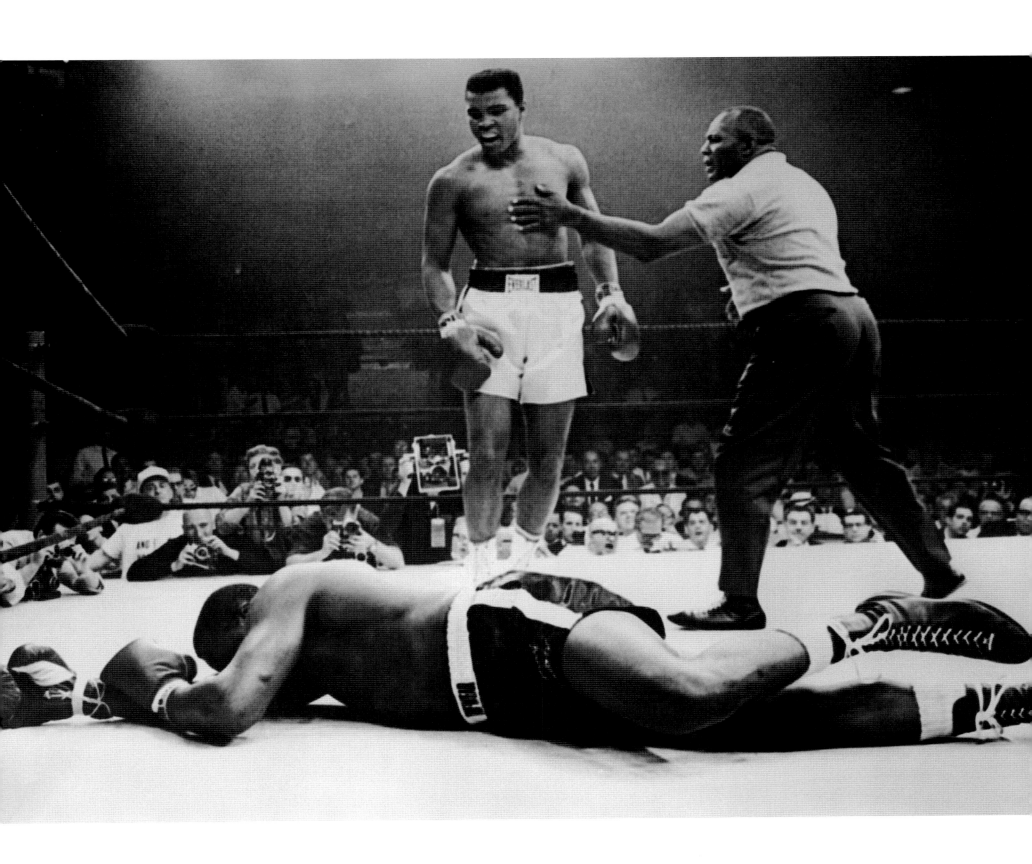

As referee Jersey Joe Walcott holds Ali back, Ali seems to gloat as he stands over Liston, taunting the downed fighter.

bum! You're supposed to be so bad! Nobody will believe this!" (This iconic tableau graced the front page of a hundred newspapers and, most famously, *Sports Illustrated*.) Jersey Joe Walcott, the referee, never even counted Liston out. A writer at ringside informed Walcott that more than ten seconds had elapsed, so Walcott declared the fight over. Ali was still the champ.

In the documentary *a.k.a. Cassius Clay*, Ali called the shot that floored Liston his "anchor punch," and he described how his downward driving fist met the forward-thrusting momentum of Liston's face after he'd thrown his own punch. He gave credit for the move to Stepin Fetchit, the black film actor who was part of Ali's entourage at the time.

DID SONNY TAKE A DIVE?

Controversy continues to this day over whether Liston threw either of the Ali fights or even both fights, and boxing historian Mike Dunne offered some interesting theories that exonerate the Big Bear.

Sonny Liston is easy to cast as a malleable mob puppet, with his connections to New York organized crime and his close relationship to Ashe Resnick, owner of the mob-controlled Thunderbird Hotel in Las Vegas where Sonny trained. But what would organized crime gain by having Liston throw either fight? Sure, in the first fight they could have bet against the favorite and gotten great odds on Clay. But, in the long run, it made more sense for them to have control of a world heavyweight title-holder than of a has-been palooka. Also, the mob had no stake in Clay/Ali, so his winning of the title would earn them nothing. Finally, no paper or money trail has ever been established to prove that the outcome was preordained.

Many boxing experts suggest that Liston was simply overconfident and therefore under-prepared for Clay. Although the Louisville Lip was undefeated, he'd clearly struggled in his two most recent bouts. Liston, on the other hand, had a sterling 35–1 record against class contenders and was rated among the top boxers to ever enter a ring. As a result of "buying into" his own press, Liston didn't train that hard for the bout and allowed Resnick to distract him with women and booze. Ultimately, he just wasn't

expecting a younger, faster, and more athletic opponent who refused to stand still.

The "blink-of-an-eye" rematch—when Liston fell to a "phantom punch" at 1:40 and refused to get up—is more problematic to decipher. Immediately after the decision was announced, the crowd started chanting, "Fix! Fix!" But was it really a crooked fight?

Liston did train hard for this one and the betting crowd made him the favorite again, so what happened? One possible answer is that Ali's hernia surgery in November, when the rematch was originally scheduled, derailed Liston's training routine. He was apparently super fit and raring to go in November, not so much in May.

Then there was the "fear" factor. After the killing of Malcolm X in February, Ali also began getting death threats. The upcoming rematch started to take on a surreal quality, and many fans feared Ali would actually be shot before their eyes. This possibility had to have had an unnerving effect on Liston. There is also the mysterious visit the Black Muslims paid to Liston before the fight—no one has ever explained what transpired.

The truth may be as simple as this: Ali was a superb, confident athlete in his youthful prime, and Liston was a hard-drinking, womanizing, thirty-plus mortal who would never again be the gladiator who annihilated Floyd Patterson.

Liston falls in the first round of his rematch with Ali, after being struck by a blow that became known as the "phantom punch."

THE SAD DEMISE OF SONNY LISTON

Liston never challenged Ali again and, after taking a year off, he went on to fight in Europe and Mexico, still knocking opponents out and managing to earn a decent living. Eventually he became a "kept man" by the Las Vegas mob, which trotted him out at parties, openings, and sporting events. Photos from those days show a fallen warrior with haunted eyes. In early January 1971, his wife returned from a trip to find his body days after his death—the victim, police reported, of an injected heroin overdose.

This was suspicious to anyone who knew Sonny; alcohol was his drug of choice, plus he was deathly phobic of needles. Even though traces of heroin by-products were found in his system, lung congestion and heart failure were listed as the official causes of death.

Ali once told author Thomas Hauser that he wished Liston were still alive so they could talk together, just a couple of old fighters discussing their careers . . . and so that Ali could tell Sonny how much he'd scared him back then.

FLOYD PATTERSON

"After the Bear comes the Hare . . ."

—ALI, ON HIS PAST FIGHT WITH LISTON AND UPCOMING FIGHT WITH PATTERSON

After Ali dispatched Liston, the next challenger on his agenda was former heavyweight champ Floyd Patterson.

This poor North Carolina boy endured a troubled childhood and then had his life turned around in a forward-thinking upstate New York reform school. From the age of fourteen, he was taken under the wing of boxing legend Cus D'Amato, who trained him to fight at the Gramercy Gym in Manhattan. At seventeen, Patterson won the Olympic gold medal as a middleweight, and then went on to box professionally as a light heavyweight and a heavyweight. When he knocked out Archie Moore in 1956 for the heavyweight title, Patterson, then twenty-one, became the youngest world heavyweight champion up to that time.

Patterson fought Sweden's Ingemar Johansson three times, losing the first match, crushing the Swede in the second, and knocking him out in the third. He was less lucky with Sonny Liston, who decked him in the first round of their first meeting, in Chicago. Patterson, whose speed seemed no match for Liston's brute force, lasted only four seconds longer in a Las Vegas follow-up bout.

But Patterson battled back—gaining victories over Eddie Machen and George Chuvalo, the latter becoming *The Ring* magazine's "Fight of the Year." Patterson was now top contender for Ali's crown, and a match was arranged for November 22, 1965, in Las Vegas.

Ali took to calling Patterson "the Rabbit," and even showed up at his training camp bearing carrots and lettuce. Unlike the scowling Liston, Patterson actually appeared amused by the champ's antics. But Patterson, always a popular fighter with white audiences (he'd been considered the "good Negro" in his bouts with Liston), was also a staunch advocate of civil rights who criticized the Black Muslims and labeled them "a menace." He also insisted on referring to Ali by his former name, Cassius Clay. This riled Ali, who started calling Patterson "Uncle Tom."

The actual fight was not much of a cliffhanger—Ali's superior height, reach, strength, speed, balance, and footwork made short work of the challenger. The champ toyed with him, scoring shots at will, yet the game Patterson lasted a grueling twelve rounds. It may not have been a thrilling fight, but it exemplified courage under pressure. Alas, not Ali's.

The crowd booed Ali for treating the boxing legend Patterson with cruelty and disrespect.

GEORGE CHUVALO

"He was the toughest guy I ever fought!"

After he retired from boxing, this respected Canadian heavyweight bragged that he'd never been knocked off his feet in ninety-three professional fights. A virtually indestructible chin and great physical resilience certainly aided him in maintaining that record. Of Croatian heritage, Chuvalo was raised in Ontario and became the Canadian amateur heavyweight champion in 1955. His string of sixteen early-round knockouts earned him the nickname "Boom Boom."

Although his 1965, close-decision loss to Floyd Patterson was voted "Fight of the Year" by *The Ring* magazine, the fighter is best remembered for his two bouts with Ali. Their first match-up occurred on March 29, 1966, in Maple Leaf Gardens, Toronto. Chuvalo went the whole fifteen rounds, but lost by a wide margin. In spite of the scoring, Ali declared that Chuvalo was "the toughest guy I ever fought." The champ reputedly suffered from sore ribs for weeks after the fight. "He never stopped coming on," added Angelo Dundee. "You've got to admire a guy like that."

In 2009, Chuvalo was featured in the 2009 documentary *Facing Ali* as one of the notable opponents who spoke about how fighting Muhammad Ali changed their lives.

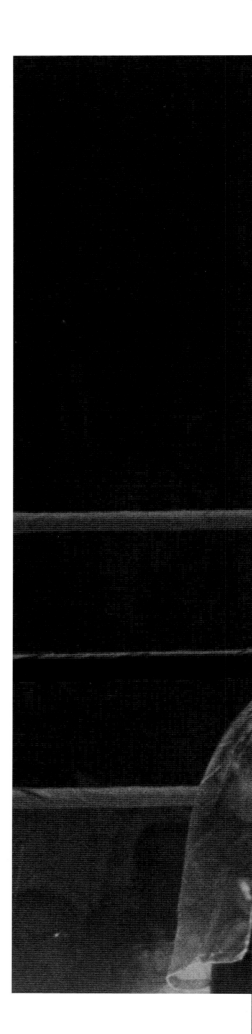

Ali sends another punishing left to Chuvalo's "cast-iron" chin.

HENRY COOPER REMATCH

"Henry always had a smile for me; a warm and embracing smile. It was always a pleasure being in Henry's company. I will miss my ole friend. He was a great fighter and a gentleman."
—ON HEARING OF HENRY COOPER'S DEATH IN 2011

In May 1966, it was off to England again for another go-round with British champion heavyweight Henry Cooper, this time at Highbury Stadium in London. Ali certainly recalled Cooper's strong left hook, which floored him in their first fight, and so kept well back from him during the bout or else held him in tight clinches. Cooper acquitted himself well, and was ahead on the scorecards in the sixth round when Ali opened up some scar tissue around Cooper's left eye. As blood poured down Cooper's face, the referee called a TKO in Ali's favor.

After retiring from boxing, Cooper became an enormously popular sports announcer and carried the distinction of being the only boxer, so far, knighted by the Queen.

Henry Cooper is covered in blood as Ali crushes him in their May 1966 rematch.

BRIAN LONDON

"I'd like a return, but only if you put a 50-pound weight on each ankle."
—BRIAN LONDON AFTER BEING KNOCKED OUT BY ALI

Brian London was another British heavyweight champion who took on Ali in 1966. His style of boxing—honest and courageous but with little finesse—earned him the nicknames "the British Bulldog" and "the Blackpool Rock." His father, Jack, had won the British heavyweight title in 1944, and his brother, Jack Junior, fought as a light heavyweight. Brian London was infamous in boxing circles for a European title fight against Dick Richardson in Wales, where both his father and brother invaded the ring to protest a head butt by Richardson when the ref called a TKO against London. Richardson's trainer had words with Brian, Brian attacked him and knocked him down, and a melee ensued.

The Ali fight was a lot less tumultuous. It took place at the Earl's Court Exhibition Hall in London on August 6, and consisted of three rounds of the champ toying with his opponent and hitting him at will. As London described the third round during a BBC interview, "he was just getting through all the time." London, not surprisingly, opted to stay in his corner and forego a fourth round.

In spite of the loss, London—who during his career had fought the top boxers of his time, including four current or former world champions—always claimed that fighting Ali was the greatest honor of his life.

Ali hits "the British Bulldog" with a devastating right. After the fight, London said he'd like a return fight with Ali, but only if the champ had "a 50-pound weight on each ankle."

Muhammad Ali with Jabir
Herbert Muhammad, son of Elijah
Muhammad, after Ali's fight against
Brian London in August 1966.

Ali on the *Eamonn Andrews Show*, with the host and other guests (from left) Lucille Ball, Robert Sharples, Dudley Moore, and Noel Coward in May 1966.

"At home I am a nice guy: but I don't want the world to know. Humble people, I've found, don't get very far."

KARL MILDENBERGER

"I don't think Ali ever had a tougher fight. Of course, he forgot all about circling away from Mildenberger's right hand and I had to remind him of it between rounds. That didn't do much good, either. As it turned out, he beat Mildenberger fighting him wrong, which I suppose is a mark of how great Ali is."

—ANGELO DUNDEE

Karl Mildenberger of Germany, the European Heavyweight Champion from 1964 to 1968, fought to retain his title six times. In September 1966, Muhammad Ali traveled to Frankfurt to take on Mildenberger, who was the first southpaw to vie for the world heavyweight title.

Before the bout, such boxing luminaries as Max Schmeling, Joe Louis, and Ingemar Johannson were introduced to the two combatants and the 45,000 fans in the Waldstadion/Radrennbahn.

When the fight began, Ali struggled to outbox the left-hander, the first he had faced as a professional. Ali seemed confused by the German's defensive posture, as noted by Howard Cosell, who was announcing the fight for the American satellite broadcast. The scoring seemed to waver between the two fighters, Ali winning a round handily, then Mildenberger roaring back. Finally, in the twelfth round, after Ali landed a series of punishing blows, the referee called a TKO against the German, whose eyes were nearly swollen shut.

September 10, 1966: Ali sends Mildenberger tumbling to the canvas in the twelfth and final round of the fifteen-round contest.

CLEVELAND WILLIAMS

Cleveland "Big Cat" Williams was a tall, wide-shouldered fighter, famous as the best boxer who never won a title. Sonny Liston, who met him twice, called Williams the hardest puncher he ever fought.

In 1965, Williams was shot several times by a policeman during a traffic stop. While the details of the shooting remain unclear, Williams nearly died, and spent much of the year recuperating from kidney damage, the loss of ten feet of small intestine, and nerve damage to his left thigh from the bullet that remained there.

In light of these injuries, it is hard to believe Williams actually met Muhammad Ali in the Houston Astrodome on November 14, 1966, to battle for the heavyweight title. Williams, with a visibly atrophied left leg, put up a gallant defense but Ali was too quick and too powerful. The three-round fight is considered by many to have been Ali's best. There were certainly plenty of people to attest to that, since the fight drew an indoor record crowd of 35,460 fans.

Sadly, in 1999, Williams was struck and killed by a hit-and-run driver.

Ali penetrates Williams's guard with a powerful left uppercut. This fight is often described as a virtuoso display of pure boxing talent. In a devastating performance, Ali dropped Williams three times in the second round and once in the third.

ERNIE TERRELL

"I think Terrell will catch hell at the sound of the bell.
He's going around saying that he's a championship-fighter,
but when he meets me he'll fall 20 pounds lighter.
He thinks that he's the real heavyweight champ
but when he meets me, he'll just be a tramp
Now I'm not sayin' that just to be funny,
But I'm fightin' Ernie because he needs the money."

Ernie Terrell was a strapping six-foot-six Mississippian whose sister, Jean, was the lead singer of the 1970s Supremes. After the World Boxing Association stripped Muhammad Ali of his title over his agreement to fight a Liston rematch, they awarded Terrell the crown in 1965 after his defeat of Eddie Machen. (Most boxing fans disregarded the WBA's ruling, since Ali had not lost the crown during a fight; the World Boxing Council also considered Ali the world champion.)

But now that a fight had been scheduled between the two men for February 1967, the question of the crown's legitimacy would soon be moot. Terrell began to refer to Ali as Cassius Clay in the press, forgetting that the tactic hadn't worked out so well for Floyd Patterson—Ali was never kind to those who taunted him with his former name. Still, when he met the champ in Houston, Terrell had no idea he would be in for fifteen rounds of public humiliation as Ali repeatedly pummeled him, yet never brutally enough for the referee to declare a TKO. "What's my name, Uncle Tom," Ali chided him between flurries of punches. "What's my name?"

Afterward, sportswriter Tex Maule declared of the fight, "It was a wonderful demonstration of boxing and a barbarous display of cruelty." When Howard Cosell protested to Ali on *Wide World of Sports* that he'd purposely hurt Terrell, Ali pointed out that it was his job to hit Terrell or else Terrell would have hit him and hurt him. Ali seemed puzzled when Cosell continued to harp on the issue.

Considering the enormous pressure Ali must have been feeling with the fateful appointment with his draft board looming (see Chapter 5), it's possible he took out some of his frustration on the unlucky Terrell.

Terrell retired from the ring in 1973 and became a music producer in Chicago.

Ali eyeballs challenger Ernie
Terrell during the weigh-in for the
title fight in Houston, Texas, on
February 6, 1967. Even on the
scales, Ali still wasn't quite as tall
as six-foot-six Terrell.

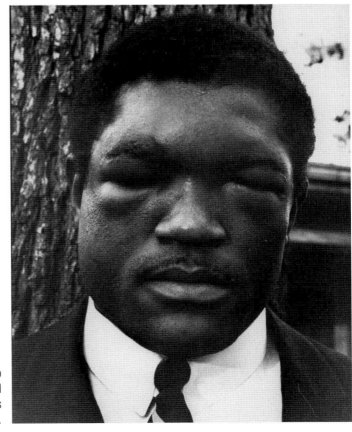

Terrell was unable to
eyeball anybody for several
days following his ruthless
pounding by the champion.

ZORA FOLLEY

A little more than a month before he was scheduled to report to the Houston induction center, Ali fought Zora Folley in New York City. Folley, a good defensive boxer with a respectable punch, had grown up in Chandler, Arizona, where he maintained lifelong ties. Although he had faced many of the same opponents as Ali—Cooper and Liston, who beat him; George Chuvalo, whom he beat; and Karl Mildenberger, whom he fought to a draw—he did not meet the champ until he was thirty-four.

A family man with nine children, Folley was such a decent guy that Ali joked he just couldn't get mad enough at him to fight him. Folley made sure to refer to Ali by his Muslim name (it's possible that press shots of Terrell's ravaged face had an impact on this decision), and Ali said later that he respected him for it and that he was a bit nervous before meeting him in the ring. The champ needn't have worried—Folley was past his prime. He gave it his best shot, but was knocked out in the seventh round.

On a somber note, in 1972 Folley was mysteriously injured in a swimming pool accident at a friend's home in Tucson. He died of severe head injuries only hours later, launching a number of conspiracy theories. Chandler, Arizona, where the fighter had been a councilman, created Zora Folley Memorial Park to honor him.

Going into the seventh round, Herbert Muhammad, Ali's manager, told him to "stop playin'." Ali dispatched Folley with two rights to gain his ninth successful title defense.

CHAPTER FIVE

CLAY V. UNITED STATES

"I ain't got no quarrel
with them Vietcong . . ."

Muhammad Ali talks with
the press on his way into
court to face trial because of
his refusal to be drafted,
Houston, Texas, June 20, 1967.

A DECADE IN TURMOIL

The 1960s in America was a time of great change and upheaval. The decade began with the assassination of John F. Kennedy (and later those of Robert Kennedy and Martin Luther King Jr.). It ended with American astronauts broadcasting from the moon. Within those historic bookends, black people marched for integration, in many cases shoulder to shoulder with whites and other races. Native Americans fought back against generations of exploitation, and young people in general grew more and more disenchanted with the government and other forms or authority. Organized marches, rallies, sits-ins, be-ins, and other protests— some peaceful, others more violent—became commonplace in streets and campuses across the nation. And underscoring all this tumult was an undeclared war, a so-called "police action," in a small Asian country called South Vietnam.

While a lot of Americans couldn't even find the place on a map, by the mid-1960s thousands of American troops were being sent to South Vietnam each month to battle the communist threat pouring in from North Vietnam. Politicians warned Americans about the "domino theory," that if South Vietnam could not hold off the Viet Cong, the whole of Southeast Asia and much of Oceania, including our allies Australia and New Zealand, could fall to communism as well.

To many black Americans, however, fear of communism was not a real concern. No, they were more troubled by the suspicion that their young men were being used as cannon fodder in this distant war—a suspicion that statistics bore out. Blacks made up approximately 11 percent of the population in the mid 1960s, yet their fatality rate in Vietnam for that same period was a shocking 14.9 percent. By 1966, more than 50 percent of blacks in America were against the war. The black soldiers themselves, frustrated by the lack of racial equality back home and angered by discrimination in their ranks, began to protest on ships and on military bases, leading to race riots in 1968.

In late 1965, these war-related issues must have seemed far away to Muhammad Ali as he focused on training for his upcoming fights. The year before he had dutifully reported to his draft board in Louisville and been declared 1Y—available for service, but only in case of war or national emergency—chiefly for the poor reading and writing skills he displayed on its tests. The heated controversy over his conversion to Islam had faded somewhat, and he was now content to be turning the world of boxing on its ear . . . and so there was nothing to make him suspect that an even greater controversy would engulf him or that he would soon become the most famous conscientious objector in history.

Child-care expert Dr. Benjamin Spock (second from left), clergyman Martin Luther King (center), unionist leader Cleveland Robinson (second from right), and black civil rights campaigner Father Frederick Reed (right) lead a March 1967 pacifist rally protesting the United States' involvement in the Vietnam War. Such peace marches as this one in New York City helped turn the tide of opinion against the war.

A CHANGE IN STATUS

"I strongly object to the fact that so many newspapers have given the American public and the world the impression that I have only two alternatives in taking this stand: either I go to jail or go to the Army. There is another alternative and that alternative is justice. If justice prevails, if my Constitutional rights are upheld, I will be forced to go neither to the Army nor jail. In the end I am confident that justice will come my way for the truth must eventually prevail."

—Ali in his official statement refusing induction to the armed forces, 1967

In early 1966, Ali received notification that the Louisville Draft Board had arbitrarily reclassified him as 1A—available for unrestricted military service—without requiring him to retake any of the tests. In a filmed interview shortly after the news broke, Ali appeared baffled and angry, questioning why he was singled out to receive a change in status. And then he dropped the bombshell. He vowed he would not serve in the United States armed forces. His religion forbade it, he said, and he therefore considered himself a conscientious objector.

"War is against the teachings of the Holy Qur'an," he explained. "I'm not trying to dodge the draft. We are not supposed to take part in no wars unless declared by Allah or the Messenger. We don't take part in Christian wars or wars of any unbelievers." He later added this widely quoted coda, "I ain't got no quarrel with them Vietcong. . . . They never called me nigger."

In March, Ali applied to be reclassified as exempt because his parents depended on him for support. He also maintained his position as a conscientious objector. His application was denied. He tried again in August, submitting a twenty-one-page letter explaining his position. Kentucky Circuit Court Judge Lawrence Grauman found for the defendant, recommending that his conscientious objector status be sustained. His ruling was overthrown by the Department of Justice, which cited an FBI report that Ali's stand was based on "political and racial grounds" rather than religious convictions and that his beliefs were a matter of "convenience."

REFUSING TO ANSWER

On April 28, 1967, Ali reported to an induction center in Houston, Texas, and three times refused to step forward when his name was called. He understood full well that failure to answer to his name was a felony and that he could be fined $10,000 and be sentenced to five years in prison. When he refused a fourth time, he was arrested.

As Ali left the induction center he encountered a crowd of supporters carrying placards and shouting, "If he don't go, we don't go!"

Even though he had not yet been tried or convicted for his actions in Houston, the New York State Boxing Commission immediately suspended Ali's boxing license and stripped him of the heavyweight title. It wasn't long before the boxing commissions in other states followed suit. Muhammad Ali was no longer the champion; he was no longer even a licensed fighter.

Once again, as they had after the announcement of his Islamic conversion, the press and the public raised a terrible clamor. The governors of Illinois and Maine officially spoke out against him, ministers and priests condemned him from the pulpit, politicians questioned his patriotism, and every armchair critic in America expressed their disgust and disappointment.

Muhammad Ali on his way into court to face trial in 1967. Ali was sentenced to five years in prison and had his championship title revoked after he was convicted of draft evasion upon his refusal to serve with the American army in Vietnam upon grounds of conscientious objection.

ALI'S DAY IN COURT

"So now I have to make a decision. Step into a billion dollars and denounce my people, or step into poverty and teach them the truth."

The case of Cassius Clay, a.k.a. Muhammad Ali, v. The United States of America went to trial on June 20, 1967. The jury took only twenty-one minutes to declare Ali guilty. He was fined $10,000 and sentenced to five years in prison. Ali's lawyers immediately filed an appeal and he was set free on bail.

There was much angry speculation among Ali supporters over why he refused to serve when he knew how harsh the penalty would be. "Why couldn't he do the right thing and just go?" many fans asked, finding it hard to believe that their hero was unpatriotic, or worse yet, a coward.

In reality (and Ali's lawyers would have been quick to tell him this), even if he'd allowed himself to be drafted, there was no chance the government would send a public figure like Ali into danger. When World War II broke out, boxing legend Joe Louis enlisted and was treated like a VIP. The army basically gave him a series of public relations' assignments, including troop visits and boxing exhibitions. It would have been no different for Ali: a few exhibition fights, a few recruitment commercials, and perhaps even a chance to defend his title while serving. Celebrities in uniform were too valuable

as agents of propaganda to risk them in combat, and so Ali would have never gone near the front lines.

And perhaps that is one reason he stood firm, because he wanted nothing to do with America's military in any way, least of all to be part of its propaganda machine. "This is his principle," Angelo Dundee said. "It's him. He's true . . . he's honest.

In an interview for *Sports Illustrated* Ali told Edwin Shrake, "I'm giving up my title, my wealth, maybe my future. Many great men have been tested for their religious beliefs. If I pass this test, I'll come out stronger than ever."

Ali would later add, "I have not lost a thing. I have gained. I have gained peace of mind."

A group of top African American athletes from different sporting disciplines, including football's Jim Brown (seated left) and basketball's Kareem Abdul Jabbar (seated right), gather to give support and hear Ali give his reasons for rejecting the draft at a meeting of the Negro Industrial and Economic Union, held in Cleveland, June 4, 1967. The decision of the Supreme Court was overturned in 1971 and Ali became a figurehead of resistance and a hero to those who denounced the war.

"He who is not
courageous enough
to take risks
will accomplish
nothing in life."

Muhammad Ali walks through
the streets with members of
the Black Panther Party in New
York City, September 1970.

HARD TIMES

"Damn the money. Damn the heavyweight championship. Damn the white people. Damn everything. I will die before I sell out my people for the white man's money."

In 1966, when Ali's commitment to the Louisville Sponsoring Group ended, he'd hired Herbert Muhammad, Elijah's son, to manage him. This, of course, earned him more flak from the media, who felt he was further turning his back on the white establishment that had fostered him.

But even with new management, things were not looking rosy for the champ once he'd lost his license. For the first time since he signed with the Louisville Group, Ali found himself with serious money problems. He had an expensive team of lawyers keeping him out of prison, plus he was paying alimony to his first wife and supporting his second wife and their new daughter. And like many celebrities in show business and sports, he had an entourage and a support staff—a lot of people who where counting on him for a paycheck. With his customary livelihood forbidden to him, Ali looked elsewhere, not only for opportunities to make money, but also for outlets to channel his enormous energy and drive.

Ali, shown here at home in Deer Lake, rarely got to relax for long—he had legal fees, alimony, and the support of his second wife and child to worry about.

A CAMPUS SENSATION

"I am America. I am the part you won't recognize, but get used to me: black, confident, cocky — my name, not yours; my religion, not yours; my goals, my own. Get used to me."

Over time, Ali found that he could make a respectable income from accepting speaking engagements around the country. His humor and personal likability never faded in the face of his legal problems, and his natural, anecdotal way of describing the black experience in America reached across racial lines and made him a hugely popular speaker at colleges and universities.

As the youth of America began to challenge their country's role in the Vietnam conflict, Ali's stand against the government earned him legions of new young fans. They saw him as a man of principle, an individual who had put his career and lifestyle on the line for something he believed in. While many black people admired him, as they did any fellow African American who bucked authority, for "standing up to the man," Ali also became one of the few lightning rods that connected liberal, educated white youth with the issues of disenfranchised black America.

Muhammad Ali, former heavy-weight boxing champion drew large crowds for his speeches, talking about civil rights, the Black Muslim faith, the Black Panther movement, and boxing with his characteristic eloquence and good humor.

This was a key moment in the evolution of Ali's life, marking his progression beyond professional sports to the country's—and eventually the world's—stage. The boxer without a license to fight had now found a new arena.

ALI ON BROADWAY

In December 1969, Ali embarked onto uncharted territory—the Great White Way. He appeared in a new Broadway musical by Oscar Brown Jr., *Buck White.* Unfortunately it only ran for seven performances, but the cast—including Ali in a Biblical beard—performed the number "We Came in Chains" on the *Ed Sullivan Show.* (During his exile from boxing, Ali was featured in a documentary, *A.K.A. Cassius Clay*, and he can be seen singing a song from the play in a section narrated by Richard Kiley.)

HOWARD COSELL: VERBAL SPARRING PARTNER

"Howard Cosell was gonna be a boxer when he was a kid—only they couldn't find a mouthpiece big enough."

One of the few broadcasters to support Ali during this controversial period was WABC's sports anchor, Howard Cosell. At a time when even the *New York Times* refused to call Ali by his Islamic name and instead continued to identify him as Cassius Clay, Cosell promised the champ he would never use his former name when interviewing him or speaking about him. Cosell eventually became a close friend of the beleaguered boxer.

The son of an accountant, Howard William Cohen was born in Winston-Salem, North Carolina, and grew up in Brooklyn. He earned a law degree from New York University, and during World War II he rose to the rank of major in the Army Transportation Corps. After the war, Cosell practiced union law in Manhattan and also represented a number of actors and athletes, including baseball great Willie Mays. When Cosell was asked to host a local radio show featuring Little League players, it signaled the beginning of his long relationship with WABC and ABC. Eventually, Cosell quit the law to become a full-time broadcaster, and—with the sponsorship of a relative's shirt company—he launched *Speaking of Sports*.

"I'M JUST TELLING IT LIKE IT IS."

From 1961 to 1974, in spite of having a "face for radio," Cosell became the New York sports anchor for WABC TV. He also began hosting a more wide-ranging radio talk show called *Speaking of Everything*.

With his brusque, in-your-face manner and knife-edged questions, Cosell's brand of sports journalism was a departure from the fawning newscasters who traditionally treated top athletes with kid gloves. Yet over the years, more and more sports reporters began to emulate Cosell's gadfly style until it became the norm. Cosell also transformed live sports coverage, with its color commentary and simple play-by-play, by incorporating a hard-nosed, analytical approach more typically seen in straight news reporting. When athletes objected to his probing interview questions, sometimes on touchy issues outside sports, Cosell would shoot back pompously, "I'm just telling it like it is."

Howard Cossell and Ali were regular verbal sparring partners over the decades and became close friends. On Ali's fiftieth birthday, Cossell gave a moving tribute, saying to Ali, "you are free to be who you want to be. I love you."

UNLIKELY FRIENDS

At first glance, a Howard Cosell–Cassius Clay friendship seemed highly unlikely . . . not with those two massive egos set on a collision course. But after they met, in 1962 when Cosell interviewed the champ for his sports roundup show, the men quickly formed a bond. Perhaps Cosell saw some trace of his personal sports hero, Jackie Robinson, in the iconoclastic young boxer. Maybe Clay was drawn to a white journalist who didn't try to hand him any B.S. Whatever the chemistry, it worked for both sides, and Cosell became part of Ali's extended entourage, first as a fight announcer, then as a friend.

"I like Howard Cosell," Ali said. "He was a professional. He knew how to bring out the best in people. He respected the law and had a sense of right and wrong and history." And, being Ali,

he naturally had to add, "But he wouldn't have been nearly as big as he was without me, and I hope he knows it."

Viewers got used to Ali's frequent TV appearances with Cosell, the two sparring playfully, and in one memorable instance, Ali pulling off Cosell's egregious hairpiece and teasingly holding it away from him. It was easy to see the affection they had for each other, even when Cosell was chastising Ali for unnecessary roughness in the ring, as he did over the Ernie Terrell fight. More often, though, they bantered amusingly without a script, the one-upmanship they each lived for their only spur. It was okay if audiences sometimes forgot, in the midst of their laughter, that they were watching (by many estimates) the most famous face in the world and the man who reinvented sports broadcasting.

LEFT: Howard Cosell at ringside.

RIGHT: Ali, listening intently to Cosell, was always ready with a riposte. Ali regularly teased Cosell for his use of "big words" and for his notorious hairpiece.

REVILED AND REVERED

"You lose nothing when fighting for a cause . . . In my mind the losers are those who don't have a cause they care about."

During his years away from the ring, Ali grew as a person in ways he never could have if he'd stayed within the narrow confines of boxing. His first moral dilemma—his conversion to Islam—led to his second moral dilemma, his refusal to serve in the army due to his religious beliefs. This in turn led to his being ridiculed, vilified, and ostracized in many circles. In time it also led to his elevation to national prominence as a representative of antiwar sentiments, black rights, religious rights, and ultimately human rights. Before he was stripped of the title, Ali was a noted American sports figure. By the time he returned to boxing, he was on his way to becoming the international Everyman.

Ali walking the streets of London

CHAPTER SIX

RETURN TO THE RING

"If my mind can conceive it, and my heart can believe it—then I can achieve it."

Ali returned to the ring in Atlanta, Georgia, on October 26, 1970, to face the "Great White Hope," Jerry Quarry.

CHANGING TIMES

By 1970, the national attitude toward Vietnam had shifted radically. Now, Americans of all ages, races, and beliefs were vehemently speaking out against the war, and Ali's refusal to serve was seen as a sign of high moral conscience. During this same period, the quest for civil rights had become a national issue. So when the people's increasing intolerance toward segregation and racial prejudice was factored in with their frustration over the ongoing war, it's no wonder Ali—always outspoken against both the treatment of blacks in American and the conflict in Vietnam—was beginning to be viewed as a political martyr by some and a hero by many.

It was in 1970 that Ali, who had not fought since the Folley match in March 1967, discovered a legal loophole that would allow him to box in Georgia, the only state without a boxing commission. Even though the governor protested, a state senator and the mayor of Atlanta saw to it that Ali was granted a license to box. The fight, against Jerry Quarry, would take place in Atlanta on October 26. Even though his case was still on appeal, Ali was back in the ring!

Not long after this match, the New York State Supreme Court determined that the fighter had been unjustly deprived of his license and so on September 28, 1970, Ali's boxing license was restored.

A COMEBACK AND A VINDICATION

Early in his comeback, Ali went on to meet—and defeat—two of the best boxers in his weight class (not taking on a bunch of palookas as some returning fighters did). He then had a date with destiny in the form of current world champion Joe Frazier.

Frazier desired the match to seal his own claim to the championship that had earlier been stripped from Ali, but he also pushed the fight because he knew Ali needed the money. Frazier had helped Ali out with occasional loans during his lean times, and he had also gone before the boxing commission to plead Ali's case.

But in spite of this, just before the match Ali started talking trash about Frazier, calling him ugly, and saying he was the champion of an oppressive white society. Frazier was flabbergasted that the man he had tried to help was attacking him so viciously. Ali later apologized to Frazier, maintaining his insults and antagonism were all for show, to build up the gate. But fight experts are quick to point out that the rivalry between these two undefeated titans was already box office gold and needed little to boost it.

Three months after Ali "met his match" with Frazier, he received some very gratifying news from his lawyers—the U.S. Supreme Court had overturned his conviction for draft evasion. Ali knew he had finally been vindicated; it was a moral victory and also a huge relief. He was "upstanding citizen Muhammad Ali" now, no longer a man with a felony conviction and the threat of prison looming over his head.

Ali training with his daughters in tow. Ali divided the nation between those who still saw him as a draft-dodger and those who hailed him as a national hero and unlikely champion of peace.

JERRY QUARRY

"Nobody has to tell me that this is a serious business. I'm not fightin' one man. I'm fighting a lot of men, showing a lot of 'em, here is one man they couldn't defeat, couldn't conquer... My mission is to bring freedom to 30 million black people."

In early 1970, Ali was able to set up a fight once again, but only in the city of Atlanta, which had granted him a license. It was there that he fought "Irish" Jerry Quarry on October 26.

Quarry was a young veteran with more than forty fights under his belt, including thirty-seven wins, when he met Ali for the first time. His family included a father and two brothers who were also boxers, although none achieved the same success Jerry had.

Although Quarry was a capable fighter, it seemed he always came up short in the big fights. When Ali was stripped of his title, Quarry was named as one of the contenders who could claim it. He defeated contender Floyd Patterson, but in 1968 he lost to Jimmy Ellis in the battle for the WBA crown. And in 1969, he lost to Joe Frazier in a fight for the New York State Athletic Commission heavyweight title. He then fought seven more bouts and won six, losing only to Canadian George Chuvalo, before stepping into the ring with Ali.

Sportswriters noted that Ali looked fit and agile—if somewhat flat-footed—in the opening round of his comeback fight, peppering Quarry with his signature jabs. Quarry, three inches shorter and pounds lighter than Ali, had a tendency to cut easily, which is what did him in that day. The fight was stopped at the end of the third round when Quarry developed a serious cut over his eye. Ali, victorious, garnered his first belt since 1967—*The Ring* magazine heavyweight title.

Ali's first fight in more than three years: he opened a cut over Quarry's left eye with a stinging right hand in the third round to finish the fight.

OSCAR BONAVENA

"My face is so pretty, you don't see a scar, which proves I'm the king of the ring by far."

The press may have called Oscar Bonavena "Ringo" because of his Beatles-style haircut, but he was no lovable moptop. He was a tough boxer and one with a temper, as well.

Bonavena started out boxing professionally in New York, building up experience and an impressive 8-0 record. But when he lost to Zora Folley in 1965, he returned to his native Argentina, where he eventually won its heavyweight crown. His occasional visits to fight in America had mixed results. He defeated George Chuvalo but lost to Joe Frazier twice—at Madison Square Garden in 1966, which cost him his Argentinian heavyweight title—then again in Philadelphia in 1968. He was also one of the contenders for the still-vacant WBA title, but lost to Jimmy Ellis in Louisville in 1967. Still, he kept fighting for the next three years, so by the time he faced Ali in New York on December 7, 1970, he'd had more than forty fights to his credit.

Bonavena was no slouch when it came to pre-fight hype—he got as much press as Ali did by trashing his opponent. And once the fifteen rounder started at the Garden, he appeared quite capable of living up to that hype. Although only five-foot-ten, he fought gamely against the six-foot-three Ali. And he would have been standing at the end had Ali not caught him with a left hook in the last round. Although Ali won the fight, it was not officially clear that he had prevailed, because, as he had done against Liston in their second fight, he stood over his opponent yelling rather than retreating to a neutral corner.

Bonavena never got a title shot again, although he kept on boxing until 1976, when he announced his retirement. That same year, he went out to Nevada, where the owner of the notorious Chicken Ranch hired him to promote some fights. Instead, Bonavena began an affair with the man's wife and after being warned to stay away from the Ranch was shot and killed by one of the owner's bodyguards. It was an ignominious end to a flamboyant life.

Ali and Argentina's notorious brawler Oscar Bonavena go eyeball to eyeball in the pre-fight medical. Ali is clearly unimpressed by his opponent's mocking grimace. Ali won the fight at the Felt Forum, New York, on a fifteenth-round technical knock-out.

JOE FRAZIER AND THE FIGHT OF THE CENTURY

Ali's first match up with Joe Frazier, which took place on March 8, 1971, at Madison Square Garden, was called the "Fight of the Century." For once, the hype preceding an Ali fight was surpassed by the actual event. Ali had fought some memorable fights before, but none had a bigger setting or such a star-studded audience—or, for that matter, such a star-studded cast. Here was Frazier, 27-0 and at the top of his game. Here was Ali, whom many believed was still the heavyweight champ, since he had not lost his title in a fight, but had it stripped away.

Joe Frazier began boxing because his parents, both boxing fans, thought he had a fighter's build—a physique he'd developed by working on the family's South Carolina farm and by using a makeshift punching bag at home. He stayed with relatives in New York to train for the annual Golden Gloves Championship and won his first title in 1962. After winning the next two, he caught the attention of the U.S. Olympic Boxing Team. He placed well enough to go to Osaka, Japan, as an alternate and, fortunately for Joe, the team's heavyweight contender, future pro boxer Buster Mathis, was injured in training. Frazier stepped in for him and won the Gold Medal for the United States.

Just as Ali had signed with a syndicate and gone right into the pro ranks following his Olympic victory, Frazier was introduced by his Olympic trainer, Yank Durham, to a group of men willing to invest in his pro career. In order to develop Frazier's skills, Durham sent Joe to California in 1966 for more seasoning. There he met with legendary trainer Eddie Futch, who set up fights for him on the coast and taught Joe the bob-and-weave style that he would use so effectively throughout his career. As he gained more experience, Frazier began to earn better competition. Jerry Quarry, Oscar Bonavena, Buster Mathis, Jimmy Ellis, and Bob Foster all fought young "Smokin' Joe" and came out second best.

Frazier began to win titles, as well. His defeat of Mathis at Madison Square Garden in 1968 won him the New York State Athletic Commission title. His defeat of Ellis at the same venue in 1970 made him the unified and unbeaten heavyweight champion, adding the WBA and WBC crowns to his collection.

And so these were the circumstances of the upcoming battle that led to the inflated hype surrounding this most historic and rarest of bouts—a test of power between two legitimate, undefeated champions who would enter the ring without a loss or a draw. Two immovable objects, two irresistible forces, coming to the mecca of boxing to face each other in a title bout unlike any ever seen before.

Fifty countries purchased rights to telecast the fight between Ali and Frazier, which was broadcast from ringside in twelve different languages. It is estimated that 300 million people around the globe watched the fight—a greater number of people than had watched the moon landing two years previously.

But this wasn't just a prizefight. It was a true New York "event," which meant that anyone who was anyone in town either had a ticket, or they schmoozed friends and associates to get one. Frank Sinatra didn't have a ticket, but he did have a camera, so he took pictures at ringside for *Life* magazine. The closed-circuit TV announcers who called the fight included Don Dunphy, who had described a thousand fights, but none as big as this one. Archie Moore, former champ (and former Ali opponent) provided color. Also assisting was none other than Burt Lancaster—actor, New Yorker, and boxing fan.

DODGING AND WEAVING

The fight began with Ali taking the early rounds. Then in the fourth round, Frazier began fighting back, and Ali started to look fatigued, as if all that time away from training during his suspension had begun to catch up with him. But he dodged and weaved his way out of serious trouble for most of the next few rounds. In the eleventh, however, Frazier pounded Ali while he was up against the ropes (although they might have kept Ali from going down).

The reinvigorated Frazier proceeded to out-duel Ali, and in the fifteenth round put the former champ on the canvas with a leaping left hook. It was the coup de grace from Frazier. Ali managed to get up, but the fight was over for him. All three judges gave the bout to Frazier. Ali had lost his first professional fight, but it wasn't for lack of trying. The effort they had made showed on their battered faces, both men

looking like a couple of "tomato cans," the disparaging term for a boxer who gets pummeled in the ring just to pull in a check, without any thought of winning. That certainly was not the case here—this was a titanic clash between the two best fighters of the time, who both gave their all to be named number one.

So Frazier came out on top that day, but it was to be a short stay for him. Two years later, after defending his title against two virtual unknowns, Frazier met yet another up-and-coming former Olympic champ, George Foreman, in Jamaica. To the surprise and shock of everyone, Foreman floored the champ six times in two rounds. This was the fight where Howard Cosell famously kept yelling, "Down goes Frazier!" He was as flabbergasted as anyone at the outcome. Frazier, who had trained and fought so hard to earn the title, lost it without putting up much of a battle.

BUSTED JAW, PART ONE

On a side note, there is evidence—an x-ray showing a quarter-inch gap—that Frazier separated Ali's jaw in the second round. Ali and his team left the Garden immediately after the bout, did no interviews, and went directly to Flower Fifth Avenue Hospital, which released the fighter after forty minutes. Ali had the x-ray taken soon after, and his jaw was later repaired in a ninety-minute operation. When asked how he had managed to keep going after sustaining an injury so early in the bout, Ali replied that in the heat of the fight he hardly felt it.

ABOVE: Jazz trumpeter Miles Davis attends the first Ali-Frazier title fight at Madison Square Garden.

BELOW: A big fan of boxing, Bob Dylan checks out the program before the big fight on March 8.

"I said a lot of things in the heat of the moment that I shouldn't have said. Called him names I shouldn't have called him. I apologize for that. I'm sorry. It was all meant to promote the fight."

Ali facing life after his first professional defeat. Ali was down but not out; he and Frazier fought twice more, with Ali winning both encounters.

JIMMY ELLIS

Ali took three-and-a-half months to recover from his wounds after the Frazier fight. He fought some exhibition matches in Dayton, Ohio, but didn't try for a title again until he faced Jimmy Ellis on July 26, 1971, in the Houston Astrodome.

Ellis was perhaps the most similar to Ali of all his opponents—a boy from Louisville who'd been inspired by his hometown champ to go into boxing. In fact, he'd actually fought Ali when they were both amateurs. Ellis hoped to go to Rome with Ali and the U.S. Olympic boxing team, but lost his qualifying match to future Light Middleweight Gold Medal Champion, Wilber McClure.

Ellis started his pro career as a middleweight, but after losing four of five bouts under trainer Bud Bruner, he retained Angelo Dundee— Ali's trainer and cornerman. Ellis began as a sparring partner for Ali, but he was soon getting heavyweight fights of his own on the same cards as the champ.

His first major fight—in Louisville in December 1967 against seasoned pro Oscar Bonavena—was a step toward the WBA World Heavyweight title recently stripped from stablemate Ali. The contest went the full twelve rounds, with Bonavena hitting the canvas in the third and tenth rounds. The unanimous decision went to Ellis, who then headed west to Oakland, where he defeated Jerry Quarry in fifteen rounds, in a "tactical masterpiece," to take the title. His first title defense took him to Sweden the following August, where he bested Floyd Patterson in fifteen rounds on points.

Throughout his career, Ellis seemed to be warming up the great heavyweights who would face Ali down the road, and his next opponent was no different—Joe Frazier, the New York State Athletic Commission's heavyweight title holder. On the line were both the WBA and WBC titles, the latter only recently vacated by Ali's opposition to the draft. Frazier was more than ready, effectively wearing down Ellis, who failed to answer the fifth-round bell after being floored twice in the fourth. Ellis went on to win three more fights, including a ten-round bout in Toronto with George Chuvalo in May, just two months before he met Ali.

The fight with Ali was a twelve-rounder for the NABF Heavyweight crown, which had been vacated when current holder, Leotis Martin, retired with an injury. Although Angelo Dundee trained both combatants, Ali gave his blessing when Dundee chose Ellis's corner. Long-time trainer Harry Wiley subbed for Dundee in Ali's crew.

As the fight started, Ali seemed like the champ of old. He looked sharp and was hitting with authority. He even did his patented shuffle. The first three rounds were pretty even, but in the fourth round Ali really turned up the heat. He tagged Ellis with a hard right to the jaw, and Ellis was never the same after that. Ali controlled the fight from then on, and with about a minute left in the final round the referee stopped the fight. Ali was actually relieved since his old sparring partner was almost out on his feet.

Jimmy Ellis training before his big fight with Ali. Angelo Dundee was Ali's trainer, but he was Ellis' trainer and manager. Dundee worked Ellis's corner for the fight because it meant a bigger share of the purse, which Ali understood completely. Ali hired Harry Wiley to be his trainer for the Ellis fight.

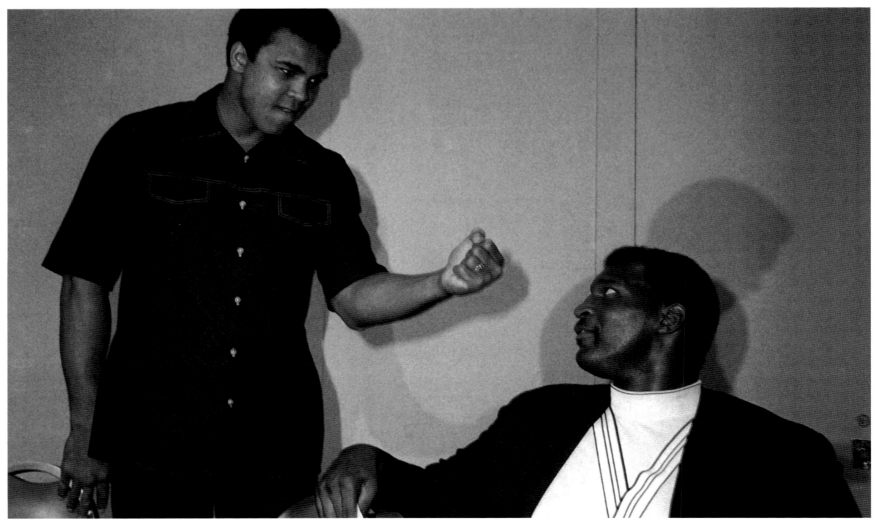

BUSTER MATHIS

"I'm a fighter. I believe in the eye-for-an-eye business. I'm no cheek turner. I got no respect for a man who won't hit back."

Buster Mathis's life and career were both short. He started out just as Ali and Frazier had, fighting well enough as an amateur to get a shot at the U.S. Olympic Team, the same 1964 team that Frazier was on. In fact, he had beaten Frazier in the trials, but when a subsequent injury made him unable to compete in Tokyo, Frazier replaced him and went on to win gold in the heavyweight division.

Mathis, who started his pro career in 1965, was gargantuan in size. His early fights saw him tipping the scales from 270 to 300 pounds. At six feet, three inches, he looked hulking, yet he had quick hands. He took off forty pounds, fighting at around 245, but still remained undefeated at 23-0. His first important fight was in 1968 against his Olympic teammate, Joe Frazier, 19-0, at Madison Square Garden, for the NYSAC title. The fight itself went eleven of fifteen rounds. Frazier took him out late in the final round for a TKO.

Mathis won five more fights, then, just before the Ali fight, lost to Quarry in a twelve-round unanimous decision in 1969, also at the Garden. Before the bout—which was to take place on November 17, 1971, in the Houston Astrodome—Ali declared, "This will be Buster's last stand. I will do to Buster what the Indians did to Custer. I'm gonna wipe him out."

It didn't quite go quite so easily, lasting twelve rounds, with Ali flooring Mathis three times in the late rounds. Ali won on a unanimous decision, and earned himself the North American Boxing Federation crown, as well.

Mathis retired after two more fights. In his post-fight years, his weight became out of control, and by the time he died in 1995, age forty-two, he weighed in at 550.

ABOVE: At six-foot-three and weighing in at up to 300 pounds, Buster Mathis was a giant by the standards of the day.

LEFT: Ali teasing Mathis before their match in 1971.

JÜRGEN BLIN

Jürgen Blin was a European fighter with a spotty resume. Although he was a somewhat impressive 27-9-6 at the time of the Ali fight, he didn't do well in title matches, losing the German BDB Heavyweight Title fight in 1968, then losing the European Heavyweight Title fight in 1970, and again in May of 1971, this time to Joe Bugner.

So stepping into the ring against Ali, Blin was what one might call "ubermatched" when compared to his opponent. During the bout on December 26, 1971, in Zurich, Switzerland, Blin managed to last into the seventh round, but went down for good about two minutes in, bloodied and bowed. Blin later said that it was a great honor to have fought Ali.

Ali and Angelo Dundee at the Hallenstadion Arena, Zurich, Switzerland, before his fight against Jürgen Blin.

MAC FOSTER

"Life is a gamble. You can get hurt. But people die in plane crashes, lose their arms and legs in car accidents. People die everyday. Same with fighters: some die; some get hurt; some go on. You just don't let yourself believe it will happen to you."

Mac Foster fought in Vietnam as a soldier and as a boxer, winning several amateur matches before being discharged and turning pro. The Fresno native fought mostly on the West Coast, building up a reputation as a powerful hitter under his trainer, Pat DiFuna.

By the time he met Jerry Quarry at Madison Square Garden in June of 1970, he had amassed a 24-0 record, all of them by KO or TKO. But Quarry was more than ready for him, getting to Foster in the fifth round, pummeling him with left hooks, then sending him through the ropes two minutes into round six and ending the bout.

Foster won four more fights before facing Ali on April 26, 1972, in Buddakon in Tokyo. Ironically, this match went the distance, a first for Foster, and without a single knockdown. He lost, though the three cards that went for Ali were not as lopsided as those in Ali's previous fights.

Foster retired in 1976 and became a youth boxing coach. He died of an infection in 2010, age sixty-eight.

ABOVE: Mac Foster at "The Noble Art" gymnasium in London.

RIGHT: Mac Foster crashes through the ropes in the sixth round during his Madison Square Garden fight with Jerry Quarry on June 17, 1970. Ali did not manage to KO Foster in the predicted fifth round of his bout with Foster in 1972.

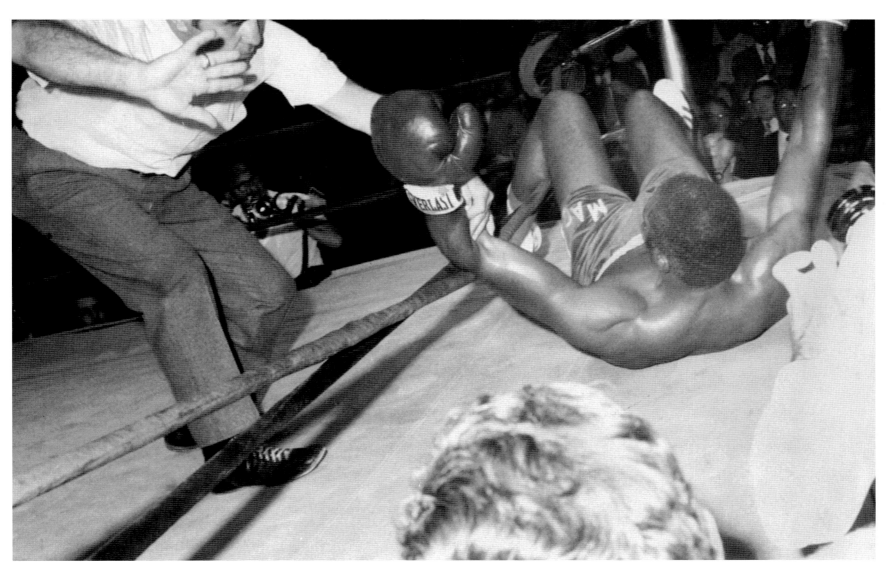

GEORGE CHUVALO REMATCH

Canadian George Chuvalo made his name boxing against fighters from America. He was a formidable opponent, hard to knock down, and able to go the distance with anyone. He was somewhat older than the other contenders, having fought in more than forty-five contests when he faced Ali for the first time in March 1966. Ali had won that fight on all three judges' cards, but he failed to knock Chuvalo down in the allotted fifteen rounds, just as so many others were unable to do.

The second match between Ali and Chuvalo was held on May 10, 1972, at the Pacific Coliseum in Vancouver. It was actually a title defense, for Ali's NABF Heavyweight title, which he'd earned by defeating Buster Mathis. Ali predicted he would actually put Chuvalo on the canvas this time, but although he failed to do so, he won the twelve-rounder by unanimous decision.

Chuvalo would have only seven more fights after this one, but he won them all, and then retired in 1978. Since then he has traveled the world, lecturing about the dangers of illegal drugs, having lost two sons to substance abuse. He was inducted into both the World Boxing Hall of Fame and the Canadian Boxing Hall of Fame.

In their rematch Ali predicted that he would knock down Chuvalo—a feat that no one else had managed. Although Ali won by decision, Chuvalo stayed on his feet throughout the fight.

FANFARE

Ali greets students at St. John's
University in New York, 1968.

"You can go to Japan, China, all the European,
African, Arabian, and South American countries,
and man, they know me. I can't name a nation
where they don't know me."

Ali gets his shoes shined as fans
gather round at Forty-Second
Street and Eighth Avenue, New
York City, in November 1971.

ABOVE LEFT: Ali playfully spars with a fan in Miami Beach, 1971.

BELOW LEFT: Photographers and fans surround Ali during a 1966 visit to a children's home in Notting Hill in London, England.

ABOVE: Muhammed Ali at his West End hotel during his stay in London to fight Henry Cooper in May 1966.

JERRY QUARRY REMATCH

"If my fans think I can do everything I say I can do, then they're crazier than I am."

To boxing fans, the night of June 27, 1972, was not as memorable for the star match-up as it was for the fight card itself. In the main bout, Jerry Quarry was set to battle Ali for a second time, two years after losing on cuts in just the third round of a fifteen-rounder fought in Atlanta. The undercard, however, featured a bout between World Light-Heavyweight Champion (and future Ali opponent) Bob Foster, who would defend his title successfully with a fourth-round KO of Mike Quarry, who was managed by his brother, Jerry.

Ali and Quarry stepped into the ring of the Las Vegas Convention Center as, respectively, the number-one and number-two contenders for the heavyweight crown, but the gap between the two was much greater than the rankings may have indicated. No one was knocked down in the scheduled twelve-rounder, but it was Ali's match to lose. He jabbed at Quarry repeatedly the whole fight, hitting him effectively with half-speed left jabs, choosing to wear down his opponent rather than finish him off quickly. The fight was stopped with less than half a minute gone in the seventh round, with a frustrated Quarry running out of breath. It was rare to see the tough Irishman overmatched in a bout, but that was the case this time.

Quarry continued to box through the 1970s. He won several more fights, including a surprising first-round TKO of hard-nosed Earnie Shavers in 1973, but lost a rematch with Joe Frazier and a bout with Ken Norton. He retired in 1977, tried a couple of comeback attempts, and then finally hung up his gloves in 1992. Later in life, he suffered from pugilistic dementia, which turned him into an invalid. He died on January 3, 1999. The same affliction would do in his brother, Mike, in 2006.

As talented as he was inside the ring, Jerry Quarry could have been the champ during a different era, but with the competition being so fierce in the 1960s and 1970s, he could get only so close.

On June 27, 1972, at the Convention Center in Las Vegas, Nevada, Ali faced the number-two contender, Jerry Quarry. On the same night, World Light Heavyweight Champion Bob Foster defended his title with a fourth-round KO of Jerry Quarry's younger brother, Mike. The evening was publicized as "The Soul Brothers versus The Quarry Brothers."

AL "BLUE" LEWIS

A fighter of some note in his day, Al "Blue" Lewis was perhaps more famous as a former sparring partner for Ali. He fought his way up the ranks of heavyweights until he started getting matches with real contenders. In October 1971, he traveled to Buenos Aires to battle the always-challenging Oscar Bonavena. Lewis lost on a disqualification, even though he had put his opponent on the canvas several times. He had given sufficient battle even in defeat, however, to earn a shot at Muhammad Ali.

The fight was scheduled for twelve rounds on July 19, 1972, in Dublin, Ireland. At first, the fight went the way one might have expected with Ali dominating, although Lewis, 27–3 when he agreed to this fight, was very game. He went down in the fifth, but managed to get himself up.

Then in the ninth round, Lewis rallied and went for it—landing blows on Ali's face and body. Ali was not only surprised, but stopped his dancing when he realized that Lewis was actually giving him a fight. Unfortunately for Lewis, he did no real damage. Ali collected his breath in the tenth, applying minimum effort to hold off Lewis, who had spent most of his energy in the previous round and had little left in the tank. In round eleven, Lewis was not wobbly, but he was almost standing still. He must have had a glazed look in his eye, because at 1:15 the referee waved his hands to stop the fight, even though the now-refreshed Ali was doing no more than jabbing and shuffling.

Lewis fought just five more times after this bout, and then retired in 1973.

Lewis trying to fend off Ali. The referee stopped the fight in the eleventh round, as Ali was putting on a dancing and jabbing exhibition and Lewis was increasingly unsteady on his legs.

FLOYD PATTERSON REMATCH

"You may talk about Sweden, you may talk about Rome,
but Rockville Center's Floyd Patterson's home.
A lot of people said that Floyd couldn't fight,
but you should have seen him on the comeback night."

—MUHAMMAD ALI

September 20, 1972, Madison Square Garden, New York—It had been nearly seven years since the first Ali-Patterson match in November 1965. That one was called in the twelfth round when Patterson ran out of gas and stopped defending himself . . . and Ali got booed for punishing a defenseless Patterson. A lot had happened to both fighters since then.

In September 1966, Patterson went to London and knocked out British champ Henry Cooper in the fourth round. He split two 1967 fights with Jerry Quarry, lost to Jimmy Ellis on points in a 1968 match held in Stockholm, and beat Oscar Bonavena by unanimous decision in a Garden match held just months before the second Ali bout. Those were the highlights of the sixteen fights Patterson had been in prior to stepping into the Garden ring with Ali on September 20, 1972.

As for Ali, the prickly Islamic convert who'd called Patterson "Uncle Tom" and "White American" had been replaced by a man who showed great respect to his opponent. The fight went seven of fifteen rounds, but the referee did not let Patterson come out for the eighth round due to a swollen left eye caused by an Ali punch in the sixth. This time around, Ali was nothing but polite to Patterson after the fight ended, calling him a "great, great" fighter. Whether Ali knew it or not, this was the "great, great" former champ's final bout.

Patterson joined the New York State Athletic Commission in the mid-1970s and remained a member until 1984. He also helped train his adopted son, Tracy, to become a fighter. Tracy was first the WBC Super Bantamweight Champion from 1992–1994, then stepped up to the next weight class and became the IBF Super Featherweight Champion in 1995. Floyd rejoined NYSAC in 1995 as commissioner, but had to resign three years later due to the onset of Alzheimer's disease. Patterson died on May 11, 2006, of Alzheimer's and prostate cancer in New Paltz, New York, where he had been living and training Tracy Patterson.

Ali throws a powerful jab to Floyd Patterson's head during their heavyweight fight on September 21, 1972, at Madison Square Garden in New York City.

BOB FOSTER

"Only a man who knows what it is like to be defeated can reach down to the bottom of his soul and come up with the extra ounce of power it takes to win when the match is even."

Bob Foster fought most of his professional life as a light heavyweight, at no more than 175 pounds. As such, he was almost unbeatable. He defeated Dick Tiger in 1968 for the WBA and WBC Light-Heavyweight crowns, which he defended numerous times. His forays into the heavyweight division, however, were not as successful. He lost to Ernie Terrell, Zora Folley, and Joe Frazier, among others. He stayed in the lower weight class in 1971–1972, and only bulked up when it was time for the fight with Ali, who was once again defending his NABF title.

When the day of the fight arrived—November 21, 1972, at the Sahara Tahoe Hotel in Nevada—Foster went in at 180 pounds, Ali at 221-plus. Foster managed to keep it close early on, even cutting Ali, a first. But the second half of this match was all Muhammad. Starting in the fifth, he knocked down his lighter opponent seven times, the last time ending the fight less than a minute into round eight.

Foster returned to the class where he was the dominant fighter, retaining both his light-heavyweight titles for two more years, until he retired from that weight class in 1974, considered by many to be the greatest of all time in that division. He went 5–2 in his last seven fights, all as a heavyweight, against no one memorable. He retired to his native Albuquerque, New Mexico, in 1978, where he became a sheriff, then a detective, earning himself the nickname "Sheriff Bob."

Foster was knocked down four times in the fifth round and twice in the seventh. After being knocked down early in the eighth, he was counted out by the referee. Nevertheless, he was the first boxer ever to cut Ali in his professional career, opening up a wound above Ali's left eye.

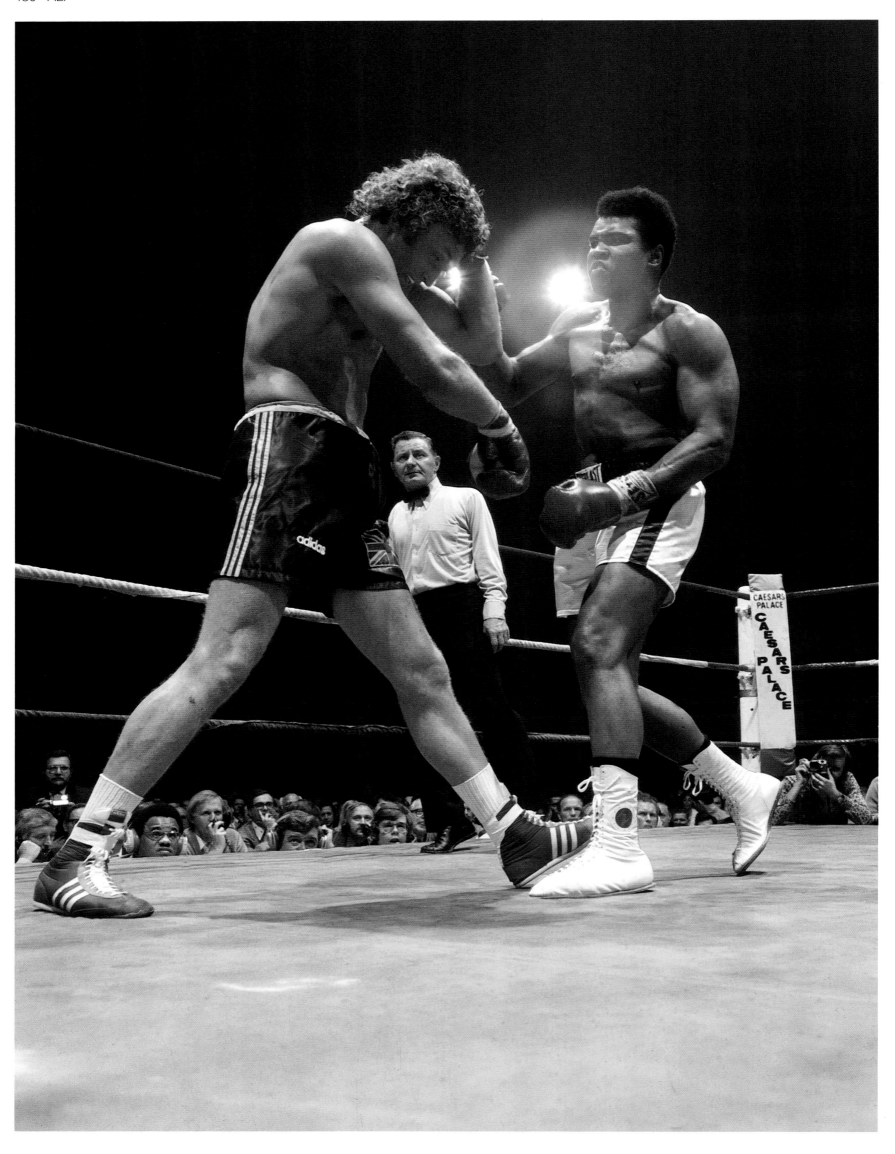

JOE BUGNER

"They can boo me, yell at me and throw peanuts at me—as long as they pay to get in."

February 14, 1973, Las Vegas Convention Center—Hungarian Joe Bugner relocated to London with his family while still a child. He began his amateur athletic career as a discus thrower, boxing just to keep fit, but soon switched to pugilism full time at the suggestion of his trainer, Andy Smith. A pro at seventeen, he was the combined British, Commonwealth, and European champ when he was just twenty-one, defeating Henry Cooper on points in March 1971. Cooper, approaching forty and a fan favorite, congratulated the new champ, and then promptly retired.

Bugner continued fighting mostly in the UK, although he did fight in Houston in 1971, defeating lefty journeyman Mike Boswell in the Astrodome by unanimous decision. His next trip to the States took him to Vegas, with a chance to face Ali, who was an 8-to-1 favorite. The fight itself was unremarkable, except that Bugner went the distance, losing by unanimous decision. Bugner went back home to London, where he promptly lost to Joe Frazier on points five months after losing to Ali the same way (Points in England are the equivalent of the three officials' card tallies in America).

But Bugner persevered; he started facing classier fighters after the Ali match—and beating them. He won his next eight fights against such notable opponents as Jimmy Ellis and Mac Foster. So by 1975, he was ready to face Ali again. Except that now his opponent was the unified WBA and WBC Heavyweight World Champion.

Ali fought the British contender Joe Bugner at the Merdeka Stadium, Kuala Lumpur, in Malaysia, before a crowd of 22,000 and won by unanimous decision.

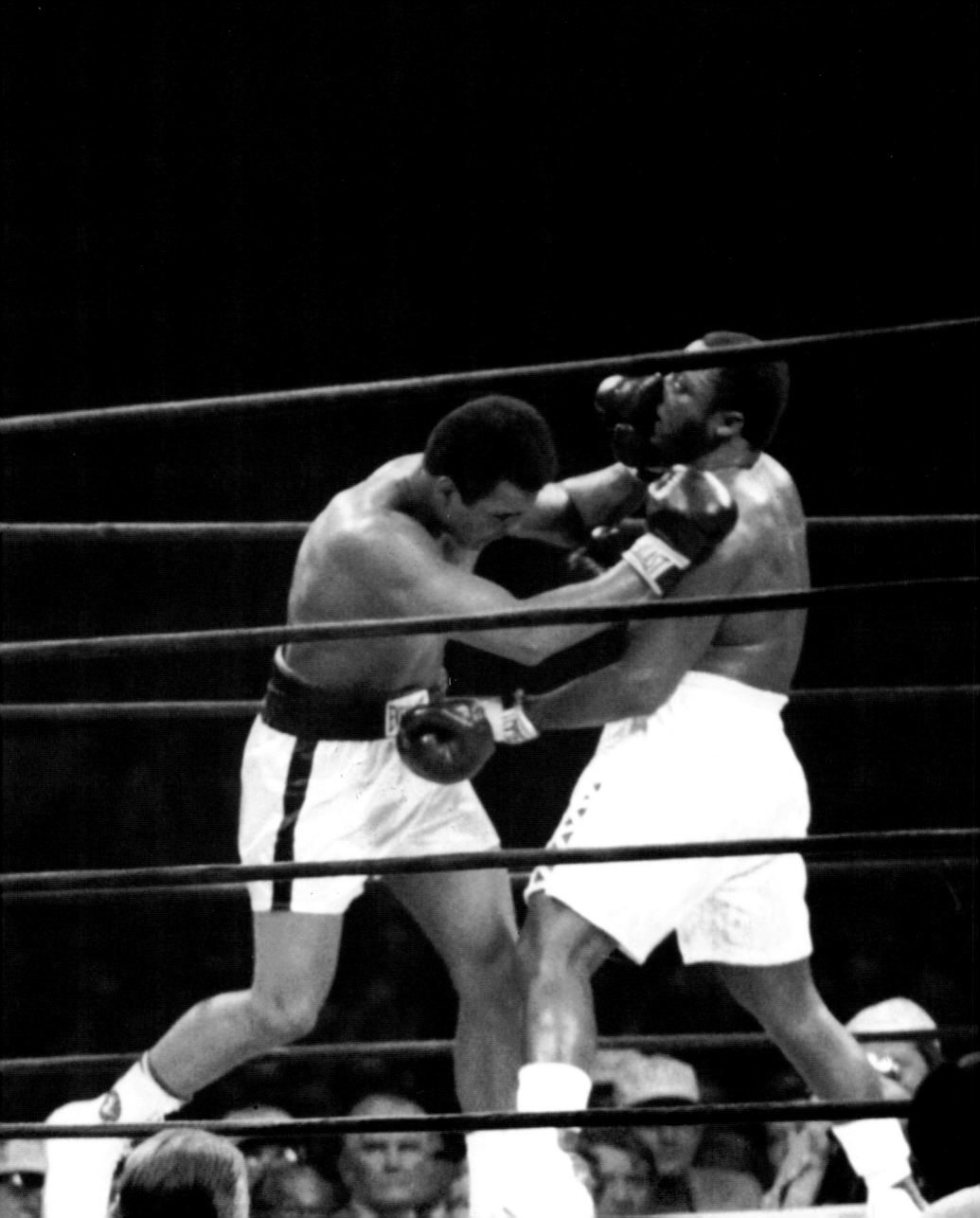

CHAPTER SEVEN

CHASING THE TITLE

"I am the astronaut of boxing. Joe Louis and Dempsey were just jet pilots. I'm in a world of my own."

The "Thrilla in Manila,"
The Ring magazine's 1975
"Fight of the Year."

KEN NORTON, THE JAW BREAKER

Illinois native Ken Norton was not your average boxer, not the sort who craved the action in the ring from an early age. Rather he came to the sport in a more roundabout manner.

In high school he'd been a superb athlete, excelling at both track and football, the latter earning him a scholarship to what is now Truman State University (formerly Northeast Missouri State). After college, Norton joined the Marines. He initially had no intention of becoming a boxer until someone pointed out that Marine boxers have their own schedule and are not subject to the standard 5:00 a.m. roll call.

After his hitch ended, he began boxing as a pro in San Diego, with most of his matches taking place against West Coast fighters. Norton had built up a perfect record of 16-0 when he lost his first fight in July 1970 to Jose Luis Garcia.

He was determined never to lose again, and, inspired by a motivational book someone had given him that stressed meditation, he won the next twelve bouts leading up to the first of what would be three matches against Muhammad Ali. And although the Ali-Frazier trio of fights are more often touted, the three Ali fought against Norton were certainly as tough, if not tougher, since Norton was as durable an opponent as Ali ever faced. Plus, the challenger's trainer, Eddie Futch, had been in Joe Frazier's corner in 1971 when Ali lost in Ali-Frazier I.

The fight took place on March 31, 1973, in the San Diego Sports Arena; Ali went into it the heavy favorite and received $210,000 of the total purse. Oddly enough, he didn't pick a round in which he would finish off the challenger. Norton, still an unknown quantity of sorts, got just $50,000, but it was a lot more than he had received in any of his other bouts. The robe Ali wore into the ring that night came from another iconic entertainer—Elvis Presley. So it seemed as though Ali would be stepping in with just another wannabe.

Yet from the start, this match would be like no other in Ali's career. For one thing, Norton was as tall as Ali, so he didn't have to punch up. And even though Ali gave the challenger all he could handle, Norton, by using his distinctive cross-arm defense, was able to fend off most of Ali's blows.

The bout went the full twelve rounds, not a first in an Ali bout. Unlike other Ali fights that went the distance, however, the scorecards were split—the referee gave it to Norton, but so did one of the side judges. Norton had won the fight, only the second loss in Ali's career. In addition, it earned Norton his first title—the NABF Heavyweight Championship. The loss also shut Ali up for a month—on doctor's orders. A blow from Norton had broken his jaw early in the bout.

He never again wore the robe he had received from Elvis.

Ali rocks Norton with a right.

"It was the end of the road as far as I could see. So many of Ali's fights had incredible symbolism, and here it was again. Ken Norton, former marine against the draft dodger in San Diego, a conservative naval town. It seemed Ali would never get his title back."

—HOWARD COSELL, AFTER THE FIRST NORTON FIGHT

THE GREATEST
AND THE KING

"People don't realize what they have till it's gone. Like President Kennedy — nobody like him. Like The Beatles, there will never be anything like them. Like my man, Elvis Presley — I was the Elvis of boxing."

It seemed inevitable that Muhammad Ali and Elvis Presley would be drawn to each other. They were both Southern-born, both from working-class backgrounds. Both had stood up for racial equality, Ali with his criticism of the government during his many speaking engagements, Elvis in songs like "In the Ghetto," and "If I Can Dream."

According to Ali, "Elvis was my close personal friend. He came to my Deer Lake training camp about two years before he died. He told us he didn't want nobody to bother us. He wanted peace and quiet and I gave him a cabin in my camp and nobody even knew it. When the cameras started watching me train, he was up on the hill sleeping in the cabin. Elvis had a robe made for me. I don't admire nobody, but Elvis Presley was the sweetest, most humble, and nicest man you'd want to know."

Ali actually replaced Elvis as a headliner after the singer's death: In October 1977, Elvis was supposed to inaugurate the Las Vegas Hilton's new Pavilion with a spectacular music show, but when he passed away before the opening, the management went after the other "greatest" and set up the Ali-Spinks fight.

THE "PEOPLE'S CHOICE" ROBE

In 1973, Elvis had a special robe made for his friend, bejeweled with rhinestones, pearls, and nailhead studs, and with the words "People's Choice" emblazoned across the back. It reputedly cost $3,000 and was designed by Bill Belew and Gene Doucette and produced by Romano of IC Costume, the team that created the King's flashy stage outfits. Elvis presented it to Ali just before the Bugner match, but Ali waited until the Ken Norton fight to show it off in the ring.

After Ali lost to Norton, he never wore the robe again, believing it had brought him bad luck. It is now a popular exhibit in the Muhammad Ali Center on Museum Row in Louisville, Kentucky.

Muhammad Ali in the robe given to him by Elvis Presley in 1973.

THAT'S ENTERTAINMENT: ALI HOBNOBS WITH CELEBRITIES

Even during his early days training in Miami, Muhammad Ali had been a magnet for celebrities. Frequently there was a famous actor or entertainer lingering ringside at the 5th Street Gym as Ali sparred, almost as though his fledgling star quality drew other, more-established stars to his inner sanctum.

As his fame increased, so too did his ability to lure celebrity fans to his fights and to his training sessions. He also began attending entertainment industry events, where he appeared thrilled to socialize with his celebrated fans.

Ali pictured with entertainer Sammy Davis Junior following his twelve-round victory against Joe Bugner in Las Vegas on February 14, 1973.

FIRST NORTON REMATCH

After Ken Norton handed Ali the second defeat
of his professional career, Ali was eager to even
the score. A rematch for the North American
Heavyweight Championship was set for
September 10, 1973, at the Los Angeles Forum.
In this bout against Norton, Ali's pride demanded
that he absolutely prove himself "the Greatest"
once more.

So he went "to the mountain" to prepare,
heading to Deer Lake, Pennsylvania, where he
trained hard every day and posed for publicity
shots chopping firewood and punching a boulder.
Whatever his real workout regimen, it succeeded
admirably. Ali showed up at the Forum a taut
212 pounds, his "speedy" weight, as the ring
announcer put it.

Naturally fans wondered how Ali's broken jaw
would hold up after fewer than five and a half
months to heal. But Ali had found an outstanding
surgeon in San Diego, a jaw specialist who
worked on wounded Vietnam vets. He assured
Ali that after his surgery "it would take a
jackhammer" to damage his repaired jaw.

Norton also appeared in tip-top shape,
the muscles of his shoulders and back rippling
in high relief. Yet his signature crablike
movements in the ring, with his right foot lagging
behind him, made him appear awkward once
the first round began. Ali quickly showed more
aggression than he had in the previous match,
out-jabbing Norton in the early rounds. The
announcer soon noted that an Ali on a mission
or with something to prove was a much more
focused fighter than when he was simply holding
onto a title. To many in the crowd, it felt like they
were watching the "old Ali."

The rematch went the full twelve rounds
ended with another split decision, this time in
Ali's favor.

Ali and Norton at a news
conference before the rematch.

"That was always the difference between Muhammad Ali and the rest of us. He came, he saw, and if he didn't entirely conquer—he came as close as anybody we are likely to see in the lifetime of this doomed generation."

—HUNTER S. THOMPSON

FRAZIER REMATCH

"Lawdy, Lawdy, I hit him with punches that would have brought down the walls of a city. He's a great and mighty champion."

—JOE FRAZIER

The second of his three fights with Frazier (bookended by the "Fight of the Century" and the "Thrilla in Manila") was a grudge match on Ali's part after Frazier toppled him and won the world title in 1971. Because it wasn't a title fight, it didn't generate much excitement at first, one sportswriter calling it a contest between two "former champions, both beaten, both past their best." The match didn't even warrant a clever marketing name from the promoters.

Before the fight, which was to be a twelve-rounder at the Garden scheduled for January 28, 1974, both boxers appeared on ABC's *Wide World of Sports* to review the first match-up. While watching the eleventh round, Ali called Frazier ignorant for thinking he had won the fight, sparking a violent response from the former champ. "Why you call me ignorant?" Frazier cried, leaping up. Ali grabbed Frazier's neck and tried to force him back into his chair. They ended up grappling and falling onto the set, and were later fined for their behavior. But the incident, and the open hostility between the two men, fanned some public interest in the fight.

During the actual match, Frazier adopted a lagging-right-leg advance, which allowed him to cut off Ali in the ring. Ali promised not to retreat to the ropes as he had done in the first fight, so the action remained fairly brisk during the early rounds. Ali even managed to keep dancing well into the middle of the fight, scoring again and again with his potent left jab. At the end of twelve rounds, Ali had won by unanimous decision.

It wasn't particularly earthshaking, just a workmanlike bout, but with Ali's defeat of Norton and now Frazier, he was free to set his sites on world champion George Foreman. This fight would get a name . . . and held the promise of returning Ali to his former fame.

RIGHT AND NEXT PAGE: The pattern for the fight was established at the opening bell: Ali circling, jabbing, and throwing combinations while Frazier bobbed and weaved attempting to get under Ali's arms and land the same left hook that had floored him in the their first fight three years earlier.

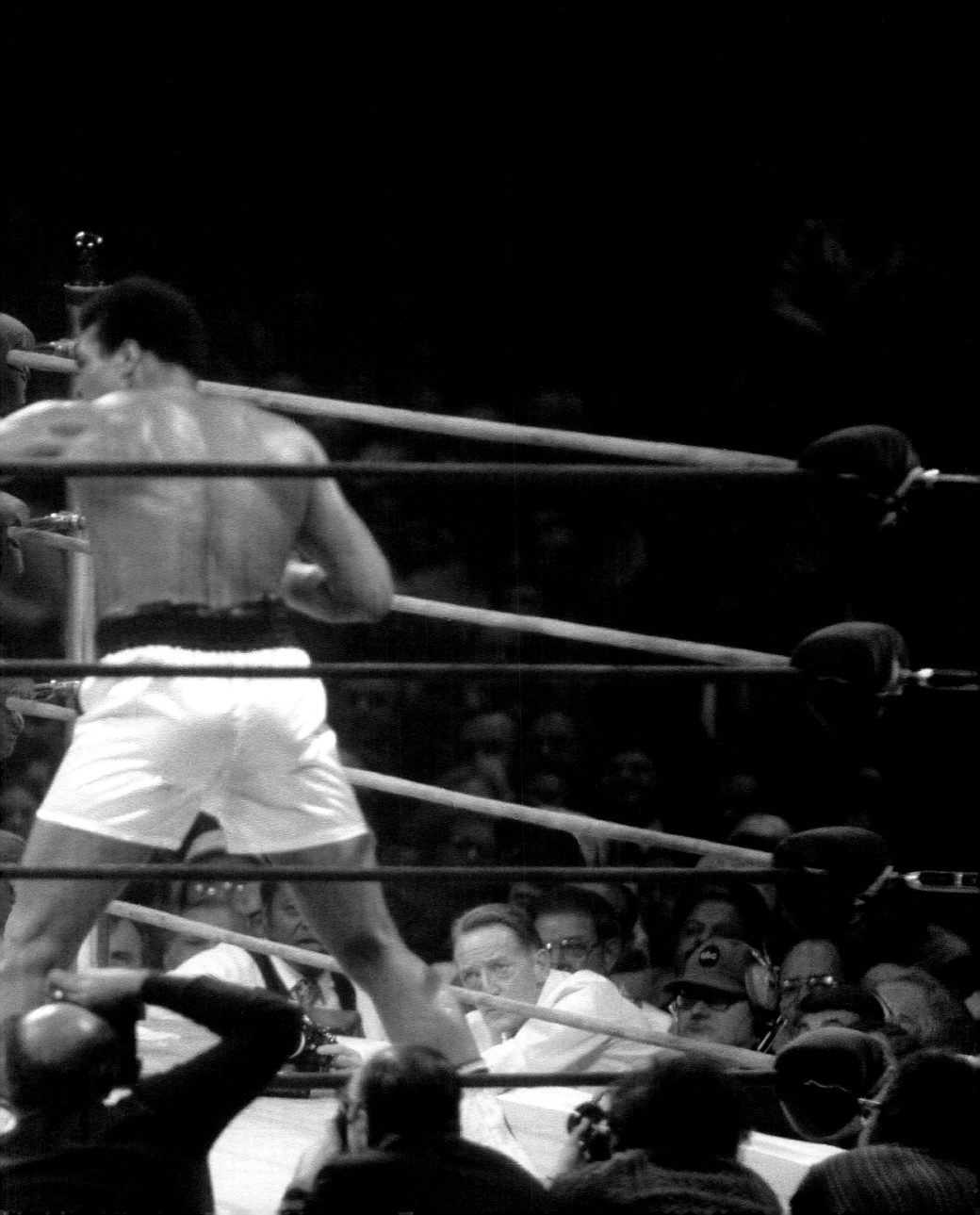

CHAPTER EIGHT

RUMBLE IN THE JUNGLE

"If you even dream of beating me, you'd better wake up and apologize."

During a stopover in Paris on his way to Kinshasa, Zaire, Ali poses with a poster for his world heavyweight championship fight against George Foreman.

GEORGE FORMAN

"If you were surprised when Nixon resigned, just watch what happens when I whup Foreman's behind!"
—Prior to 1974 fight against George Foreman

Ali's next bout would be a historic prizefighting spectacle set in the heart of Africa with the World Heavyweight title at stake. His opponent was the current champion, George Foreman, a young, six-foot-four tower of terror who boasted a 40–0 record, including an awe-inspiring thirty-seven knockouts. The fight was christened the "Rumble in the Jungle," and it gained worldwide interest right from the start.

Even though Texas-born George Foreman became the 1968 Olympic heavyweight gold medalist , in Olympic boxing, he was no clean-cut athletic role model. He admits he'd been a troubled teen whose behavioral problems stayed with him into his adult life.

He turned professional in 1969, and after thirteen fights he counted thirteen victories, eleven of them by KO. In 1970, as he progressed doggedly toward the heavyweight title, the results were pretty much the same—twelve wins, no losses, eleven knockouts. He even bested Canadian iron man George Chuvalo with a TKO in the third. By the end of 1971, after seven straight wins, all by KO or TKO, Foreman was ranked the number-one contender by both the WBA and WBC. He continued his streak in 1972 with five straight knockouts, and fight fans grew increasingly eager for a world-title bout.

Ali emerged dancing in the first round and caught Foreman several times, but it was impossible for Ali to keep dancing for long in the oppressive heat of Zaire.

SMOKING JOE FRAZIER

Foreman was finally set to meet undisputed and undefeated World Heavyweight Champion Joe Frazier in Jamaica on January 22, 1973. In the late 1960s, Frazier had taken a pass on the scramble for Ali's vacated title, but he had ascended to the throne just the same by beating champ Jimmy Ellis for the crown, and then holding off Ali himself in 1971.

Frazier appeared unbeatable to much of the boxing world—so "Big George" Foreman, in spite of his own outstanding record, came to the "Sunshine Showdown" a three-to-one underdog.

In a matter of minutes, however, the crowd and commentators witnessed a jaw-dropping turnaround, as Foreman's potent combinations decked Frazier six times in the first two rounds. Howard Cosell, part of HBO Boxing's first TV special, broadcast his own incredulity across the airwaves with a repeated litany of "Down goes Frazier! Down goes Frazier!"

And although Frazier managed to rise every time, after the second knockdown his balance and motor skills were affected. The referee called the fight before the gruesome second round was even over. George Foreman had proven that his record was no fluke; he was now the undisputed heavyweight champ. But he also suspected that it wouldn't be long before an aging former champ would come gunning for him.

SPORTIN' WITH NORTON

In the meantime, Foreman had an easy take down of Puerto Rican José Roman in Tokyo—in under two minutes—one of the fastest knockouts in heavyweight boxing history. Next came a more serious challenger, former NBAF title-holder Ken Norton. Norton had a powerful punch, an effective cross-arm defense, and a unique crablike way of advancing. Furthermore, he was almost never in trouble in the ring, even when he lost on points, as he had done with Ali the second time.

Foreman had clearly studied his opponent; he stayed back from Norton's long reach until he saw an opening near the end of the first round, and then he clocked Norton so hard he fell to the canvas. When Norton rose, he was still shaken. After three more knockdowns by Foreman in the second, the fight was stopped. Foreman later explained that he knew once Norton got some momentum, he was hard to beat. "I didn't want him to get into the fight."

Unlike Ali, who had charmed the press and the public when he was world champion, Foreman appeared aloof and antisocial, barely even acknowledging the media. Years later Foreman explained that he was following the example of the dour Sonny Liston, whom he had sparred for on occasion.

THE FIGHT IS DELAYED

The much-anticipated Ali-Forman match-up was set for September 1974 at the Mai 20 Stadium in Kinshasa, capital of the emerging African nation of Zaire (now the Democratic Republic of the Congo). Promoters immediately proclaimed it "the Rumble in the Jungle."

Both fighters arrived during the summer, chiefly to accustom themselves to the equatorial heat and humidity, but Foreman's eye was cut while training, and the fight was moved ahead to October. The cut prevented him from sparring, causing him to declare that this was the best thing to happen to Ali, since Foreman "had to get ready for the fight without being able to box."

Naturally, Ali spent a good amount of time during the delay touring the country and drumming up support from the locals. The Oscar-winning documentary *When We Were Kings* (1996) shows a hyped-up Ali eagerly glad-handing the populace. And he never missed a chance to taunt Foreman, creating his trademark rhymes and reciting for the press, "We're gonna get it *onnn*, because we don't get *alonnng*."

Ali speaking to the press in Kinshasa before the fight.

THE FIGHT

"Now you see me, now you don't. George thinks he will, but I know he won't!"

—Muhammad Ali

On October 30, the day of the fight, Ali entered the stadium as the underdog. It was not unexpected; Foreman had demolished Frazier and Norton, the only two fighters who had ever beaten Ali—even if Ali had later evened the score with both men.

But shortly before the fight, Ali announced to trainer Dundee that he had a plan to defuse Foreman. He knew the champ was used to short fights; only one of his previous twelve opponents had lasted beyond the second round. Ali figured if he could somehow blunt Foreman's powerhouse punches over a long-enough period of time, the big fighter would tire. And he had an idea of how to make that happen, something photographer George Zalinsky had suggested. If only it would work . . .

At least the 60,000 Zairois in the crowd were on Ali's side, chanting *"Ali bomaye!"* ("Ali, kill him!") as he stepped into the ring.

In the first round, Ali came out aggressively, landing direct, right-hand punches with no set-up, hoping to disorient Foreman. But George soon began to return fire, tagging Ali a number of times. It was during the second round that Ali turned to his secret plan—leaning back against the ropes with his arms protecting his body, letting Foreman pummel him with little effect—a tactic Ali would later term "rope-a-dope."

Meanwhile, Ali kept sneaking in head shots, enough so that Foreman's face began to swell. Ali also utilized his patented "clinch lean," forcing Foreman's head down with a glove at the back of his neck, and resting his weight on the other fighter's shoulders.

Ali's team (along with the referee) congratulate him on regaining the title of heavyweight boxing champion.

"IS THAT ALL YOU GOT?"

"Don't watch Ali's gloves, arms, or legs
when he's fighting. Watch his brains."

—JOSE TORRES

Perhaps most damaging of all, at least psychologically, was Ali's constant challenging taunts, egging Foreman to throw more punches, whenever the two were in a clinch. Foreman continued to hammer blows upon his opponent but soon began realize he was having little effect. In the fourth and fifth rounds, an Ali combination staggered Foreman, who appeared to be increasingly losing steam.

Near the end of the fight, after Foreman walloped Ali with a massive body blow, Ali hissed, "Is that all you got, George?" to which Foreman replied after a pause, "Yep . . . that's about it." Ali knew he owned the fight from then on.

A weakened Foreman again tried to pin Ali to the ropes in round eight, but Ali retaliated with a series of right hooks and a five-punch combination, followed by a left hook that raised Foreman's head into position for a devastating right to the face. Foreman faltered, tumbling onto the mat, and then struggled to regain his feet.

But the referee had counted him out before he was able to rise completely.

Ali had vindicated himself on a number of scores. He'd shown that he could take a punch (video footage of the fight showed Foreman striking hundreds of blows); he'd demonstrated that he could alter his style of boxing to best almost any type of fighter; and he'd proved to the world at large that he was once again the Greatest. He was now undisputed world champion, holder of the WBA, WBC, and the Ring heavyweight titles.

Foreman claimed in his autobiography, *God in My Corner*, that on the day of the fight the water he normally drank before a bout tasted odd. He suspected it had some "medicine" or "drugs" in it. But when he complained in the dressing room, his trainer denied anything was wrong. Foreman still insists that someone on his team had been working for the other side. Most fight analysts believe Foreman simply wasn't in peak condition and that Ali outmaneuvered him.

George Foreman later became famous for making multiple boxing comebacks, usually to help support his George Foreman Youth Center in Houston. He had a religious epiphany in 1977 after a undergoing a near-death experience in his dressing room and afterward became a born-again Christian and an ordained minister.

In the 1990s, Foreman began a new career as a TV spokesman for car mufflers. Not long after, he was approached to lend his name to a lackluster seller, a clam-shaped electric grill. He agreed, and the revamped George Foreman Lean Mean Fat-Reducing Grilling Machine went on to sell more than 100 million units, earning the fighter an estimated $200 million.

After the "Rumble," Foreman and Ali became friends. An especially poignant moment occurred after the documentary *When We Were Kings* won the 1996 Academy Award—Foreman, on his way to join the group on stage accepting the award, stopped to help Ali up the steps.

Foreman went on to make multiple comebacks of his own and built up a hugely successful business empire.

ROPE-A-DOPE

This was Ali's supreme survival tactic. Cultivated as a necessity during the Rumble in the Jungle with hard-hitting George Foreman, he utilized it occasionally in later fights. Welterweight Manny Pacquiao also employed it to beat Miguel Cotto, and Argentine boxer Nicolino Locche used it throughout his career as "El Intocable," the Untouchable One. Another fan of rope-a-dope was "Irish" Mickey Ward, who turned to it in the latter part of his career when it helped him win a welterweight championship.

According to Angelo Dundee, the idea for the strategy—a boxer leaning back against the elastic ropes and letting them absorb much of a punch's energy—came from photographer George Kalinsky. He had suggested that Ali become "sort of a dope on the ropes, letting Foreman swing away, but . . . hit nothing but air." Publicist John Condon refined the expression to "rope-a-dope."

But regardless of who came up with the concept, its use in the bout was indicative of one of Ali's greatest strengths: his ability to outwit opponents he couldn't necessarily out-punch. Some critics considered these unorthodox methods—his dancing, retreating footwork; the

Ali shuffle; and now rope-a-dope—almost a form of cheating, "boxing outside the box," as it were. But in the end, it all came down to what boxing analysts call "ring generalship," that is, the ability to control the pace and the flow of a fight. Ali showed enormous ring generalship in many of his fights, but never more so than in Zaire.

Writer George Plimpton, who was part of the press corps in Zaire, would go on to include the fight in his book *Shadowbox*. He described Ali on the ropes as "a man leaning out his window trying to see something on his roof." (Writer Normal Mailer was also part of the press corps and described the match in his book *The Fight*, his take on black American culture. Hunter S. Thompson, who had been sent by *Rolling Stone* to cover the fight, apparently never left the hotel pool or, one assumes, the tiki bar, and so never sent in a report.

After the fight, Foreman's team accused trainer Angelo Dundee of loosening the ropes to give Ali more room to sway away from Foreman's attack. Dundee always swore he did nothing to the ropes, that it was the intense heat that loosened them, but controversy over the matter continues to this day.

At the end of the second round of the "Rumble," Ali's trainer, Angelo Dundee begged Ali to stay off the ropes, but Ali waved him away, insisting, "I know what I'm doing. Later, Ali explained, "Dancing all night, my legs would have got tired. And George was following me too close, cutting off the ring. In the first round, I used more energy staying away from him than he used chasing me."

"Last night I had a dream,
When I got to Africa,
I had one hell of a rumble.
I had to beat Tarzan's behind first,
For claiming to be King of the Jungle.
For this fight, I've wrestled with alligators,
I've tussled with a whale.
I done handcuffed lightning
And thrown thunder in jail.
You know I'm bad.
Just last week, I murdered a rock,
Injured a stone, Hospitalized a brick.
I'm so mean, I make medicine sick.
I'm so fast, man,
I can run through a hurricane and don't get wet.
When George Foreman meets me,
He'll pay his debt.
I can drown the drink of water, and kill a dead tree.
Wait till you see Muhammad Ali."

—PRIOR TO 1974 FIGHT WITH GEORGE FOREMAN

Ali in training for his epic
battle with Foreman.

DON KING, PROMOTER

In a sport already full of loud, colorful, and outrageous characters, the brash, polarizing boxing promoter Don King still manages to stand out. With his signature gray "troll doll" hair and often-splashy clothing, he is a hard man to miss.

Cleveland native King managed to overcome a rocky start in his adult life, including running an illegal bookmaking parlor, committing two homicides thirteen years apart, and serving four years in prison for the second infraction, which had been knocked down to non-negligent manslaughter.

King first got involved in boxing when he asked Muhammad Ali to fight in a charity exhibition in support of a Cleveland hospital. He then formed a partnership with experienced fight promoter Don Elbaum, who oversaw a stable of fighters working in the Cleveland area.

In 1974, King got a huge break . . . he was able to outmaneuver a rival promoter and negotiate a $10 million purse—the highest up to that time—for the Ali-Foreman fight. Originally he had gotten Ali and Foreman to sign contracts saying they would fight for him if he could promise them $5 million each. He then began looking for a country that would pay big bucks to gain the prestige of a world-class fight. President Mobutu Sésé Seko wanted the fight held in Zaire and was so eager for the resultant publicity, he agreed to the sky-high price.

Meanwhile, King had put together a consortium composed of the Panamanian company Risnelia Investment, the British Hemdale Film Corporation, Video Techniques of New York, and his own Don King Productions to handle all the details involved in bringing the "Rumble in the Jungle" to a waiting world. The televised fight became one of the biggest media events of the decade and King received much of the credit. He then secured his position as a top fight promoter by arranging the third Ali-Frazier fight, another media blowout, which he called the "Thrilla in Manila."

Ali (right) with the Rev. Jesse Jackson (left) and Don King (center). The Rumble in the Jungle was Don King's first big venture as a boxing promoter. He managed to get both Ali and Foreman to agree to let him promote the fight by promising them $5 million each.

"Martin Luther King took us to
the mountaintop: I want to take
us to the bank."

—DON KING

In addition to promoting fights, King also began to manage fighters under the aegis of Don King Productions. His roster included some of the top boxers of the 1970s: Larry Holmes, Wilfred Benîtez, Roberto Duran, Salvator Sanchez, and Wilfredo Gomez.

For the next two decades King continued his winning streak, promoting the likes of Mike Tyson, Evander Holyfield, Julio César Chavez, Aaron Pryor, Bernard Hopkins, Ricardo Lopez, Félix Trinidad, Terry Norris, Carlos Zarate, Andrzej Golota, and Marco Antonio Barrera. In 1984, he even managed the Jackson's Victory Tour.

CRIMINAL TIES AND LAWSUITS

But all was not rosy in the King Empire. Rumors hinted of his ties to crime syndicates, while King was forced to plead the Fifth Amendment before the Senate when asked about his connection to mob boss John Gotti.

There was also growing dissatisfaction among his flock of fighters. Ali sued him in 1982 for underpaying him more than a million dollars for the Holmes fight. Holmes himself accused King of bilking him out of more than $10 million over the course of his fighting career. Former world champion Mike Tyson sued the promoter for $100 million, claiming he had repeatedly cheated him out of millions; the suit was settled out of court for $14 million. Tyson said of King: "[He] is a wretched, slimy, reptilian motherf*****. This is supposed to be my 'black brother' right? He's just a bad man, a real bad man. He would kill his own mother for a dollar."

In spite of his uneasy relationships with some of his fighters, King continues to promote matches, often on late-night talk shows, where he is a popular guest.

King himself sued ESPN for $2.5 billion, claiming a documentary it had made about him was biased, focusing as it did on his involvement in the two homicides, plus his threats to break Larry Holmes's legs and other unsavory behavior. The case was thrown out of court on the basis that King couldn't show "actual malice" on the part of ESPN.

When he is not stirring things up in the boxing world, King relishes quiet time with his family, including five grandchildren, and each year keeps up with his tradition of giving away two thousand Christmas turkeys to needy South Floridians.

The Rumble was just as big a victory for promoter Don King as it was for Ali.

SPORTSMAN OF THE YEAR

"I hated every minute of training, but I said, "Don't quit. Suffer now and live the rest of your life as a champion."

After Ali's hard-fought, emotional victory in Zaire, it is not surprising that the editors of *Sports Illustrated* voted him their 1974 Sportsman of the Year.

The award, one of the most prestigious in the world of sports, is presented each year to an individual or team whose achievements exemplify, in character and performance, the ideals of sportsmanship. Other recipients include Roger Bannister, Stan Musial, Rafer Johnson, Arnold Palmer, Bill Russell, Bobby Orr, Billie Jean King, Jackie Stewart, Chris Evert, Michael Jordan, Wayne Gretzky, Tiger Woods, the Boston Red Sox, Brett Favre, Michael Phelps, and Derek Jeter.

The award itself is a ceramic urn that depicts Greek athletes. The recipient also receives a cover story in the magazine; in Ali's case the cover showed the champ sporting a dapper tuxedo and a natty red carnation.

That same year, Ali was also awarded the Hickok Belt as top professional athlete.

Ali raises his arms in victory as a stunned George Foreman is led back to his corner.

CHAPTER NINE

STATESIDE AGAIN

"It's lack of faith that makes people afraid of meeting challenges, and I believed in myself."

Ali was back. He went on to win
ten straight title defenses.

CHUCK WEPNER: "GIVE THE WHITE GUY A BREAK."

"A man who has swallowed more blood than Dracula."

—ANONYMOUS QUIP ABOUT WEPNER

Chuck Wepner, a son of working-class Bayonne, New Jersey, made his professional boxing debut in 1964, after boxing in the Marine Corps and working as a club bouncer.

In the early part of his career, Wepner toted up a majority of wins amid occasional losses, and in 1967 he won the vacant New Jersey heavyweight title at the Jersey City Armory. He'd always been a popular, if somewhat crude, fighter in the Northeast Boxing Club circuit and was soon competing in the big leagues, going up against George Foreman (for a loss in the third by KO) and Sonny Liston (a loss in the tenth by KO). After the latter fight, Wepner required more than 120 stitches; it was no fluke that his nickname was the Bayonne Bleeder.

But Wepner battled back, as the grittiest fighters do, and after a knockout loss to Bugner in England, he managed to win nine of his next eleven bouts, besting former WBA champ Ernie Terrell along the way. He was now in a position to take on Muhammad Ali . . . for the glory of the challenge, if not exactly for the world heavyweight title. (Wepner was not a WBC top-ten contender, so the title was not at stake, but Don King promoted the bout as if it were.)

Ali was guaranteed $1.5 million to fight, and Wepner was offered $100,000, considerably more than he'd ever earned before. Both men agreed, and the bout, billed as "Give the White Guy a Break," was scheduled for March 24, 1975, at the Richfield Coliseum in Cleveland, Ohio, with an undercard featuring Foreman vs. Bonavena. The event—the first major boxing match held in Cleveland since Schmeling-Stribling in 1931—would be broadcast throughout the world.

Chuck headed for the Catskill Mountains in New York State to train for eight weeks under the watchful eye of manager Al Braverman and trainer and cutman Bill Prezant. Wepner, who maintained a day job as a liquor salesman, told reporters he'd never before had a chance to train full time. The reporters, in turn, wondered if Wepner thought he could actually survive the fight. Wepner shot back that he'd been a survivor his whole life . . . and that if he could survive the Marines he could survive Ali.

For his part, Ali—who had seen firsthand how badly Liston damaged Wepner in 1970—promised not to hit the challenger in his cut-prone face if he could help it. Whether this

Chuck Wepner jokingly aims a jab at Muhammad Ali during a press conference before their fight scheduled for March 24 in Cleveland.

was his true intention or just part of the pre-fight build-up is hard to tell. During the fifteen rounder, Ali showed little to no hesitation in wailing on Wepner's face.

When he arrived in Cleveland ten days before the fight, Ali was noticeably out of shape; he toned up by jogging through the city's Metroparks.

The bout began with the two fighters sizing each other up, but then Wepner began pressing Ali. Ali retreated, playing rope-a-dope, but Wepner's blows kept glancing off Ali's raised gloves, hitting him on the back of the neck (an illegal rabbit punch). Ali called several times for the referee to intervene, and when he didn't Ali grabbed Wepner and starting tattooing his neck with intent. This happened several times throughout the fight, Wepner rabbit-punching, and Ali retaliating.

Ali maintained control for most of the middle rounds, but in the ninth round Wepner caught Ali off guard with a shot to the ribs and sent him tumbling backward onto the mat—only the third time Ali had been floored in his pro career.

The fight announcers weren't buying it, however, crying, "A knockdown or a push?" and insisting that Ali had either tripped over his own feet or was simply off balance when Wepner struck. (Some claimed Wepner had his foot on Ali's toe.) At the end of that round, Ali took command, delivering jab after jab to the bleeding Wepner. But Wepner refused to give up, and the bout staggered on until the fifteenth round. With nineteen seconds to go, the referee stopped the fight when Wepner sank onto the ropes in sheer exhaustion.

Whatever else can be said about Chuck Wepner's legacy as a fighter, he was seconds away from going the distance with the Greatest. "I gave Ali a good fight," he insisted.

ROCKY: THE REAL STORY?

"And if I can go that distance, ya see, and that bell rings, ya know, and I'm still standin', I'm gonna know for the first time in my life, ya see, that I weren't just another bum from the neighborhood."

— ROCKY BALBOA TO ADRIAN, *ROCKY*

Chuck Wepner's boxing career contained so many ups and downs and turnarounds—plus the ultimate underdog fight—it would not have been at all surprising if someone had appropriated his story and made it into Hollywood movie.

As it turns out, someone did . . . at least according to Wepner, who spent years trying to prove it. It troubled him deeply, this usurping of his life and fight career by a stranger, and it continued to bother him even while he did time in prison for drug possession.

When Wepner battled Ali in Ohio, a young actor named Sylvester Stallone saw the fight on closed circuit in California. He had done a few films, been given second or third leads, but he knew he needed something really big, a breakout role, to make it in Hollywood. After watching the Ohio bout—where a white, small-town boxer got his shot at going the distance with the loud-mouthed, flamboyant black champion—he decided it would make a rousing movie screenplay. In addition, there would be a

wonderful lead role, a lovable lug named Rocky, that Stallone could play in his sleep (which some filmgoers thought was exactly the case).

And so the *Rocky* franchise was born, earning a Best Picture Academy Award for the original film and big box office receipts for most of the four sequels.

Chuck Wepner was certainly aware that *Rocky* was based on his own story. How could he not have been? When he went to see the movie in a Manhattan theater, word got out that he was in the audience, and when the film ended, he received a standing ovation. Friends told him he should sue Stallone or at least demand some kind of restitution. But Wepner claimed he didn't want money, just an acknowledgment from Stallone that the screenplay was based on his fight with Ali. (Supporters of Stallone counter that the movie is closer to the story of boxer Rocky Graziano, whose real name, Rocco Barbella, was clearly the inspiration for "Rocky Balboa.")

Sylvester Stallone, as Rocky Balboa, faces Carl Weathers, as Apollo Creed, in a scene from the blockbuster movie *Rocky*, directed by John G Avildson.

But Stallone, who had early on admitted to reporters that he had loosely based the character of Rocky on Wepner, now denied any connection between the celluloid boxer and the real boxer. Still, as a peace offering, he gave Wepner a chance to be in *Rocky II*, playing a fighter named Chink Weber. Unfortunately, Wepner botched his screen test, and Chink got written out.

In 1976, Wepner climbed into the ring to face Andre the Giant (as the undercard to Ali's exhibition match with Japanese wrestler Antonio Inoki). Andre pick him up, spun him around, and tossed him into the crowd. Imagine Wepner's surprise when that exact scene was replicated in *Rocky III* between Stallone and the towering Hulk Hogan as Thunderlips. Again, Stallone's reps denied any connection to Wepner. "This guy keeps using my life," Chuck lamented.

When he started partying a little too hard with local mob friends, Wepner's life went downhill, and in 1988 he was arrested for cocaine possession. While Chuck was serving time in Northern State Prison in Newark, Stallone arrived to film *Lock Up* and made a point to visit the fighter. But Wepner still wasn't satisfied, so once he got out of jail, he contacted a lawyer and sued the actor. Stallone eventually settled out of court, and Wepner received an undisclosed sum.

An ESPN documentary, *The Real Rocky*, which details this long battle of wills, was first shown in October 2011. (A film biography called *The Bleeder* is also supposedly in the works.)

In June 2011, Sylvester Stallone was inducted into the International Boxing Hall of Fame. Chuck Wepner, one of only three fighters to knock down Muhammad Ali, is not in the Hall of Fame.

RON LYLE

Ron Lyle is considered one of the best heavyweight boxers who never won a title. His fans knew, however, that the hard-punching Denver native would never disappoint them.

Lyle was one of nineteen children, and as a teen was arrested for taking part in a gang-related murder. While in prison, he was knifed, and during the seven-hour emergency surgery he "died" twice on the table. After he recovered, the prison's athletic director, Lt. Cliff Mattax got him interested in boxing. He was paroled after seven and a half years and started boxing at the Denver Elks Gym and eventually ended up on the U.S. Boxing Team.

At the age of thirty, relatively late for a boxer, he turned pro and soon boasted a 19-0-2 record with seventeen knockouts. His streak ended with a lost decision to a top-form Jerry Quarry. Then came another eleven wins and one draw, followed by a loss to the talented Jimmy Young.

Lyle's next fight was challenging Muhammad Ali for the title on May 16, 1975, at the Las Vegas Convention Center. Ali was coming off a relatively easy win against Wepner, but he'd also been knocked down in that fight, so he was understandably cautious, especially because Lyle was quite aggressive in the early rounds. Ali coasted in the center of the ring, covered up and allowing Lyle to score off him. Lyle, to his credit,

did not get lured into a game of rope-a-dope when Ali tried to engage him there.

By the middle of the bout, Ali was behind in points, but he also seemed to be controlling the pace of the fight, picking and choosing his shots. Then in the eleventh round Ali nailed Lyle with a strong right, followed by a swift series of punches. Lyle appeared dazed, apparently unable to defend himself. Yet when the referee called the fight, Lyle's corner could not believe it. When their fighter was interviewed after the match, there didn't seem to be a mark on him.

Lyle went on to fight George Foreman in what would become one of boxing's most thrilling and brutal matches. Early in the fight, Lyle walloped Foreman's torso so hard that his trunks nearly fell down. He also floored him twice in the fourth round, only the third man, besides Ali and Young, to accomplish that feat. Foreman had his revenge in the fifth round when he won by a knockout.

In his heyday, Lyle scored victories over Oscar Bonavena and Ernie Shavers and won a split decision over Joe Bugner in 1977, but after that he eventually began taking on fringe fighters. He retired, made several tepid comebacks, faced another murder charge, was acquitted, and then ran a boxing gym in Denver. He died in November 2011 from a stomach ailment.

Ali lands a devastating left hook to Ron Lyle's jaw during the eleventh round of their fight on May 16, 1975, in Las Vegas, Nevada. Ali had been behind on two of the three scorecards and even on the third, but a barrage of punches in the eleventh round sent Lyle reeling and assured victory for Ali.

BUGNER REMATCH

"I say get an education. Become an electrician, a mechanic, a doctor, a lawyer — anything but a fighter. In this trade, it's the managers that make the money and last the longest."

By 1975, Joe Bugner had paved the way for an Ali rematch—and title bout—by besting eight straight opponents, including top-tier fighters like Jimmy Ellis and Mac Foster as well as some of Europe's best heavyweights. The fight was set for June 30 of that year in Merdeka Stadium in Kuala Lampur.

This choice of an outdoor, tropical venue might have been the seed of Bugner's undoing, however, since the humidity and heat were both fierce that day. For fifteen rounds Ali dominated the fight, keeping Bugner on the defensive, although the Brit stayed on his feet to the end.

Still, his lackluster performance and loss by a unanimous decision earned him the scorn of fans. It was only in a 2008 interview that Bugner explained how the fierce temperatures in the stadium had pole-axed him, forcing him into a defensive position.

Bugner retired in 1976, but like many of his compatriots, made several comebacks. He moved to Australia in 1986, began fighting as "Aussie Joe," and actually won the Australian heavyweight title in 1995. When he retired for good in 1999, his record stood at 69-13-1, with a total of forty-three knockouts.

Ali dominated the fight against Joe Bugner but did not knock him down.

THE WIVES OF ALI

Muhammad Ali was married four times and fathered seven daughters and two sons. Two of his girls, Miya, born in 1972, and Khaliah, born in 1974, were from two different extramarital relationships.

SONJI ROI CLAY

Ali married Sonji Roi, a cocktail waitress and aspiring singer, in Gary, Indiana, on August 14, 1964, after a courtship of less than a month. Ali said the toughest fight he ever had was with his first wife. The conflict came down to the fact that Sonji, whom Ali wed before he converted to Islam, would neither convert nor conform to that religion's strict marriage laws or clothing restrictions. They divorced in 1966. There were no children.

Sonji Clay-Grover went on to record a number of songs in the 1970s, such as "Here I Am and Here I Stay," that got airplay on Chicago-area radio stations and can now be heard on YouTube. She recently died in her South Side Chicago home at the age of 59.

BELINDA BOYD/KHALILAH ALI

Muhammad Ali married Belinda Boyd in Chicago on August 17, 1967, soon after the suspension of his boxing license. Unlike his first wife, Belinda was the child of Islamic parents and had no need to convert. After marrying Ali, she changed her name to Khalilah.

Ali had first met Belinda, age ten, at the Muhammad University of Islam (a grade school), when she asked for his autograph. When he next

Clay's first wife, Sonji Roi, in 1965, after their separation.

"I got him on the downstroke."
—Khalilah Ali, on her life
with Ali during his exile from boxing

saw her, she'd become a tall, striking teenager working at a Chicago bakery; he expressed his interest to a Muslim friend who made the introduction. Belinda's parents arranged the marriage—the couple never dated, Ali just came for dinner. Khalilah said of their odd courtship, "I really didn't care. I figured he was tall enough and good-looking enough." Love soon blossomed on her part, however, and together they had three daughters, Maryum, born in 1968; twins Rasheda and Jamillah, born in 1970; and one son, Ibn Muhammad, born in 1972.

In 1975 Ali, who was known to stray, began a serious affair that would eventually end the marriage in 1977. According to Khalilah, he had met beautiful LA resident Veronica Porsche at the Salt Lake City Airport and invited her to the Rumble in the Jungle in Zaire. When Porsche arrived in Kinshasa, Khalilah quickly figured out why she was there and threw a fit. But soon Veronica was traveling with Ali's entourage, explained away, variously, as Belinda's traveling companion, Ali's cousin, the baby-sitter, and a close family friend. Ali even started introducing Veronica as his second wife (Muslim tradition allows him four).

Discord over Veronica again erupted in 1976, with a public hotel quarrel between Khalilah and Ali, were in the Philippines for the Thrilla in Manila. Afterward, Khalilah and her four children relocated to Chicago apartment a mile from Ali's own residence. There she began working as a publicity agent and photographer for *Bilalian News*, the official Muslim newspaper. In interviews dating from that time, she refused to discuss her husband, preferring to focus on her own endeavors.

After her divorce from Ali, she found work in Chicago as a stage actress, but a move to Hollywood earned her only bit parts. She remarried and divorced three times, bearing another set of twin daughters with her fourth husband, Rene Gonzalez Camacho, a man she truly loved, but who was an unstable Vietnam vet affected by Agent Orange.

As of 2011, Khalilah Camacho-Ali was working the lunch shift at Mount Sinai Hospital's elegant Founder's Room in Miami Beach. Tall and engaging as always, she still carries the cane given to her by the president of Zaire. "No matter what," she says of Ali, "we will always be friends."

VERONICA PORSCHE ALI

Veronica Porsche was born in Louisiana, but grew up Echo Park, a suburb of Los Angeles, and attended the University of Southern California. The dark-haired beauty was only eighteen in 1974 when she traveled to Zaire to be one of the four poster-girls promoting the Rumble in the Jungle. Ali began an affair with her at the time, made her part of his retinue, and finally married her in Los Angeles in 1977, after his divorce from second wife, Khalilah, was finalized.

He and Veronica had two daughters: author Hana Yasmeen Ali, a writer, and actress and undefeated professional boxer Laila Ali. The couple divorced in 1986. Their marriage broke apart because they eventually acquired separate interests and began to move in separate directions. After the divorce, Veronica expressed a desire to become a model in Paris.

In 1992, Veronica married jazz vocalist Carl Anderson, best known for portraying Judas in the Broadway production and the film version of *Jesus Christ Superstar*. In 2004, Anderson died of leukemia.

YOLANDA "LONNIE" WILLIAMS ALI

In 1964, when Yolanda Williams was nearly six years old, a well-known twenty-two-year-old boxer named Cassius Clay came home to Louisville for a photo shoot. Some neighborhood children, including a pigtailed Yolanda, went along to be photographed with the fighter. Those photos showed a young girl mesmerized by Clay, while he had her seated right next to him in several shots. They were occasionally in touch after that—she said he encouraged her to stay in high school and do well. Flash forward nearly two decades, and Clay, now Muhammad Ali, finds himself in a relationship with that same girl, who has become a successful businesswoman.

A 1978 graduate of Vanderbilt University, Yolanda Williams planned to become a clinical psychologist, and she initially took a job with Kraft Foods to earn money for her graduate degree. Her time at Kraft inclined her to switch to an MBA program, which she decided to pursue at UCLA Anderson. She'd seen Ali briefly in Louisville in the early 1980s, and while on the West Coast, she reconnected with Ali, who was also living in Los Angeles at the time. She remembered him as "this beautiful, very charismatic athlete—a Greek god almost," and recalled that she had been in love with him when she was seventeen.

By the time they were in LA together, Ali was already exhibiting early symptoms of Parkinson's syndrome—the hand tremors and slurred speech. Yolanda began to look after him while she studied to complete her degree. Her pursuit of that MBA became their "shared dream." And after the two married in 1986—the same year she earned her degree—she turned her skills to becoming the brand manager for what she calls "Corporate Ali." Not only did she streamline her husband's wide-ranging business affairs, she was also instrumental in the planning and building of the Muhammad Ali Center, a museum and education complex in Louisville.

The Alis have one son, Asaad Amin, who was adopted in 1996 aged five.

Jacqueline Kennedy Onassis greets Muhammad Ali and his third wife, Veronica, at the Robert F. Kennedy Tennis Tournament in New York on August 26, 1977. Proceeds from the 1977 charity affair went to underprivileged children.

"A man who views the world the same at fifty as he did at twenty has wasted thirty years of his life."

"Age is whatever you think it is. You are as old as you think you are."

"Friendship . . . is not something you learn in school. But if you haven't learned the meaning of friendship, you really haven't learned anything."

"It isn't the mountains ahead to climb that wear you out; it's the pebble in your shoe."

CHAPTER TEN

THE THRILLA IN MANILA

"Joe Frazier, I'll tell the world right now, brings out the best in me. I'm gonna tell ya, that's one helluva man, and God bless him. He is the greatest fighter of all times, next to me."

—ALI, AFTER THE THIRD REMATCH

Ali regretted some of the uncharacteristically cruel comments he made about Frazier before their first fight. He was far more respectful after their third meeting.

THE THRILLA IN MANILA

The third Muhammad Ali–Joe Frazier match-up took place on October 1, 1975, at the Araneta Coliseum in Quezon City, Metro Manila, in the Philippines. Promoter Don King promptly labeled it, the "Thrilla in Manila." And a thriller it was, from its heated lead-up, with Ali again tossing verbal trash at Frazier, to its domestic woes (Ali and wife Khalilah quarreling in public), to the fight itself, which many fans consider one of the best bouts of the twentieth century.

The Ali-Frazier scorecard was tied at one apiece as they came to Manila four and half years since their last meeting: Frazier won in 1971, while Ali came out on top in 1974 with a TKO. But the rivalry and antagonism between the two fighters never waned—mostly, it must be said, due to Ali's continual harassment of a man who went to bat for him during his days in exile—and so this fight was to be the grudge match to end all grudge matches. (Too bad Ali spent more time exercising his mouth than his body; he was in less-than-peak shape when he arrived in Manila.)

Philippine president Ferdinand Marcos had lobbied for the fight to be held in his country, hoping it would provide a smokescreen for the unrest already brewing there. When Ali and his entourage, the "Ali Circus," arrived—including Veronica Porsche—they set up a relaxed training camp. Ali and his crew were convinced that

Frazier was far past his prime, and subsequently Ali trained lightly, preferring to spend time with Porsche, whom he introduced to Marcos as his wife (this infraction was the basis, supposedly, of the widely reported quarrel with his real wife at the time, Khalilah, who flew in from the States to berate him).

Frazier, meanwhile, trained like a man possessed. And perhaps he was, by the specter of an opponent he'd more than once tried to help, and who continued to call him "gorilla" and other demeaning names in the press.

"WHUPPIN' ON JOE"

The fight was scheduled for 10:45 in the morning so that it could be broadcast live during prime time in other parts of the world. Ali predicted that he would "put a whuppin' on Joe," and as the bell rang for the first round, he proceeded to do just that, jabbing at will and winning on points. Frazier, meanwhile, stayed low, trying to avoid Ali's punishing left, while attempting to get in body blows of his own. Round Two found Ali playing rope-a-dope, working Frazier's head, while Frazier continued to assault Ali's midsection. At one point the referee warned Ali for holding Frazier's neck—a rare occurrence because most refs blithely overlooked this bad habit of the champ's.

Ali: "They told me you was all washed up."
Frazier: "They told you wrong, pretty boy."

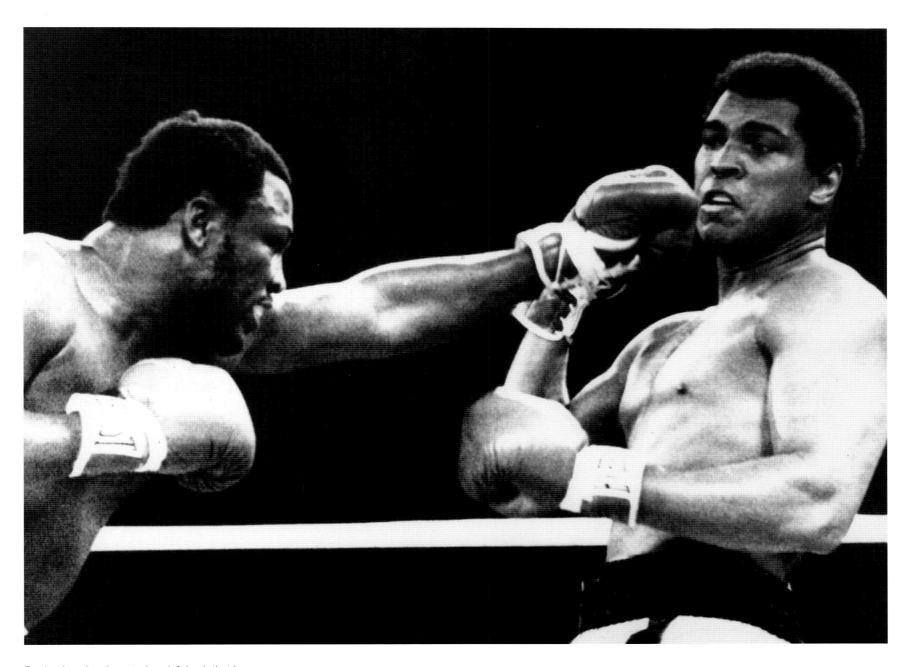

Frazier throwing the notorious left hook that he
had used to devastating effect in so many fights
previously. Promoted by Don King, the Thrilla in
Manila was broadcast to sixty-eight countries
worldwide. Ali earned about $9 million and Frazier
made approximately $5 million.

NEXT PAGE: Ali swings and misses with a right hook.

THE FIGHT

In the third round, Ali began stretching out his left arm, holding Frazier off like a cartoon bully taunting a little kid. Whenever Ali went to the ropes, Frazier would precisely aim his body shots, not swinging crude roundhouses as Foreman had done. Then, suddenly, Ali rallied, springing away from the ropes and pounding Frazier, again and again. It was a breathtaking combination of boxing science and targeted aggression.

But Ali paid a price, showing noticeable weariness in the next few rounds; even allowing Frazier to tag him with a solid left hook in the fifth. In Round Six, Frazier looked like he was taking control of the fight, and so Ali started dancing, making Joe work to get near him. During the seventh round, Ali muttered, "Joe, they told me you was all washed up." Frazier snarled, "They told you wrong, pretty boy." Joe continued to dominate his opponent during those middle rounds, undaunted by Ali's furious combinations and antic movement. It seemed possible to many that Frazier might carry the day—that Ali's indifferent prep work and the intense heat inside the arena would do him in.

A SECOND WIND

Then, during Round Ten, Frazier began to slow down and Ali got his second wind, peppering Joe with a series of combinations, leaving him with badly swollen eyes. During the next few rounds, Frazier gradually lost the ability to see, and meanwhile, Ali kept up his assault. By the fourteenth round, Frazier was virtually blind, and Ali, almost too weary to carry on, still managed to administer further punishment.

When Frazier staggered back to his corner, trainer Eddie Futch knew he had to stop the fight. "I want him, boss," Frazier protested. Futch soothed his fighter, telling him that it was all over, but adding that no one would ever forget what he'd done that day. Meanwhile, in his corner, Ali was telling Angelo to cut off his gloves, that he'd had enough. The surprise on Ali's face was apparent when Futch threw in the towel; it could just as easily have been Angelo ending it.

Ali later said it was the closest he'd ever come to dying.

The fight became legendary almost over night. ESPN ranked it as the fifth greatest sporting event of the twentieth century. A shopping center erected next to the Araneta Stadium was named Ali Mall in honor of the victor.

In the tenth round, Frazier began to tire, and Ali turned the tide, using his speed and agility to dance more and to unload a series of fast combinations, swelling Frazier's eyes to the point that nothing but a tiny slit remained open.

JEAN-PIERRE COOPMAN

It's a fairly good indicator that a champion fighter is past his prime when he starts to ask for easy competition. But in Ali's case, it was more likely he was still recuperating from the grueling Frazier fight in Manila when he agreed to a title fight with a "lightweight" heavyweight Belgian boxer named Jean-Pierre Coopman. For this bout on February 20, 1976, Ali was tipping the scales at 226, not his speedy weight, plus he was just getting over a cold and had been disrupted by a fire at his hotel, but ultimately it didn't matter one bit—he could have been in a full-body cast and still prevailed.

Coopman, called the Lion of Flanders, was a former cyclist and soccer player who reputedly built up his physique as a stonecutter before he began boxing professionally. At the time of this bout, he was ranked No. 1 in Europe, but to anyone who saw the fight, which was held at the Roberto Clemente Stadium in Puerto Rico, it appeared that Coopman couldn't throw a punch and could barely take one. Whenever Ali got him in a clinch, it looked like he was testing his opponent's strength, and then thrusting him away in disdain.

Two minutes into the fifteen rounder, the Belgian's left eye was already starting to swell from Ali's repeated jabs. This cakewalk for the champ lasted five rounds, and ended when Ali hammered the Belgian with five combinations in a row for the knockout. Showing great sportsmanship, Ali immediately went to the young boxer and put an arm over his shoulder. Ali said afterward that the fight had been harder than it looked, that Coopman was "awkward and could take a lot of punches." In spite of that, analysts viewed the Coopman match as little more than a sparring session for Ali—so untalented was the opposition—yet to be fair the Belgian did go on to win the European championship with his defeat of Basque Urtain.

There were stories circulating at the time that Coopman was out partying and drinking the night before the match, celebrating his upcoming meeting with the great Ali, a circumstance that might explain his uninspired performance. Whatever the cause, the "Lion" never got to roar that day.

Coopman later dabbled in movies and in 2007 was creating paintings of legendary boxers.

Ali knocks out Coopman in the fifth round. Ali later said, "It ain't nothing to brag about. He ain't a great fighter."

BOOED AT BUDOKAN

At a reception in April 1975, Muhammad Ali was introduced to Ichiro Hatta, president of the Japanese Amateur Wrestling Association. Ali, with his typical lack of finesse, asked Hatta, "Isn't there an Oriental fighter who can challenge me?" Ali even said he would give this person a million dollars if he won.

His challenge made headlines back in Japan, and Antonio Inoki took him up on it. Inoki was a professional wrestler who had begun staging bouts against champions of other martial arts with the aim of proving that wrestling was the superior discipline. His financial backers offered Ali $6 million for the fight. Ali agreed to their terms in March 1976, and the match was scheduled for June 26 at the Nippon Budokan arena in Tokyo.

Behind the scenes, there was a lot of Japanese anger toward America's President Nixon for taking the dollar off the gold standard, which resulted in the massive appreciation of the yen and the ruination of the Japanese export market. Ali didn't help things any when he debarked from his plane and started crowing, "There will be no Pearl Harbor! Muhammad Ali has returned!"

The upcoming fight was at least drawing a lot of attention; it would be broadcast to thirty-four countries to an estimated 1.4 billion viewers. In Shea Stadium the Japanese telecast would be the main event on a card featuring a live exhibition bout between gargantuan wrestler, Andre the Giant, and boxer Chuck Wepner, the Bayonne Bleeder. Sports just didn't get any classier than this.

Ali entered into the spirit of the event, asking Inoki when they should rehearse. Inoki shook his head. This was not an exhibition, he explained. This was to be a real fight. Then Ali saw Inoki sparring—throwing his opponent and delivering violent dropkicks and vicious grapples—and he realized he might be in over his head. Ali's reps renegotiated the rules, insisting that Inoki forego the dropkicks, throws, and grapples.

INOKI GETS HIS KICKS

The actual fight was something of a travesty. Inoki, who excelled at the art of hooking and shooting, spent most of it on his back, kicking at Ali's legs. At one point Ali actually leapt up onto the ropes to protect his thighs. He didn't throw a punch until the seventh round, and only managed six punches during the entire fight. Meanwhile, he had a swollen, bleeding wound on his left leg. The public criticized Inoki for how he conducted the fight, but few people knew that his right leg, his kicking leg, was broken.

At the end of fifteen rounds, Inoki was up by three points, but they were deducted for fouls. So the match ended up a draw, each fighter able to save face. But that might have been difficult, considering the crowd began booing and chanting, "Money back! Money back!" and started lobbing garbage into the ring.

The fight proved a lasting embarrassment for the great Muhammad Ali (the less-great Chuck Wepner also suffered his own personal low back in Flushing, when Andre raised him up and heaved him right out of the ring). Ali's leg wound would later become infected, and he developed two blood clots that impaired his mobility for the rest of his career.

Yet in spite of the viciousness of the fight, Ali and Inoki became good friends. Inoki, who actually borrowed the fighter's theme from the movie *Ali*, wrestled for another twenty-some years, and in 1998 Ali flew to Japan to view his final match.

Ironically, this bizarre fight is regarded by many as the precursor to the current form of ring combat known as mixed martial arts.

Inoki aims an illegal dropkick at Ali during the exhibition match at Nippon Budokan

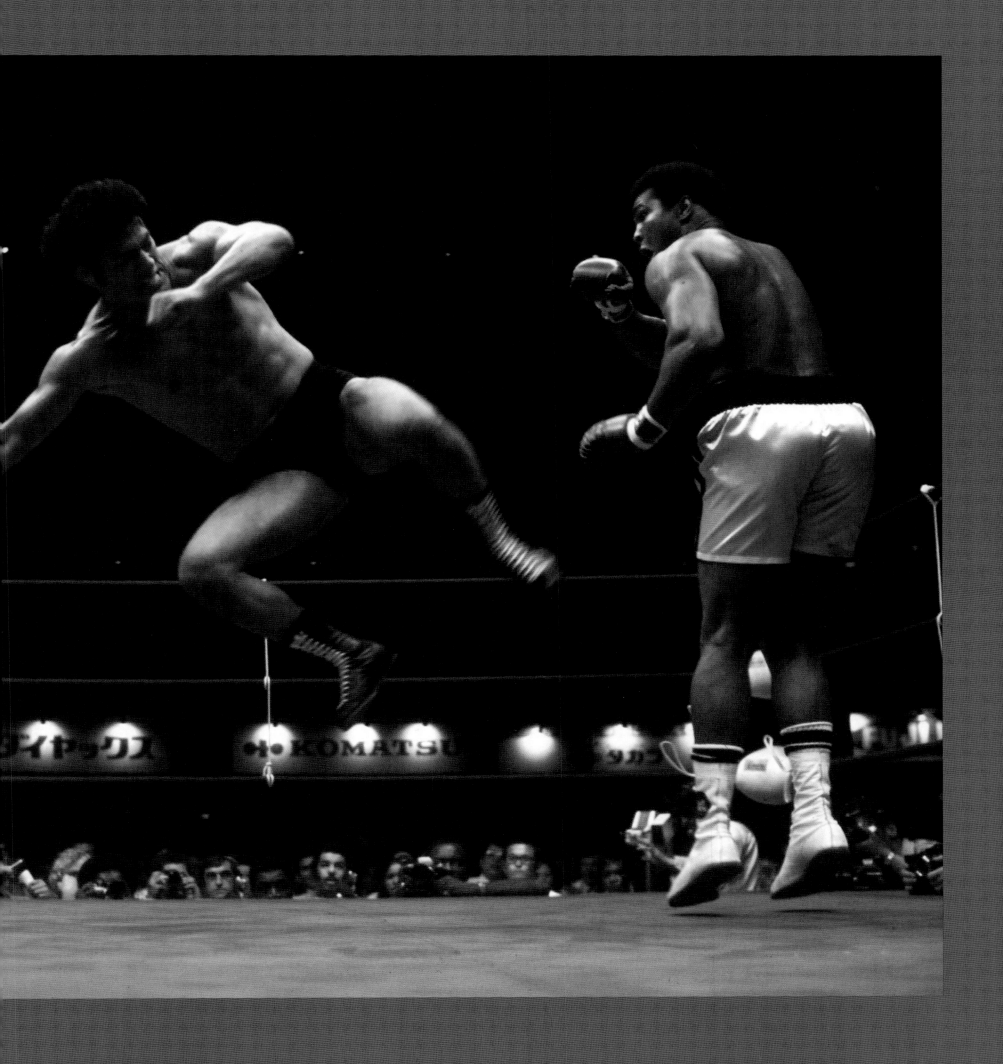

JIMMY YOUNG

"When you can whip any man in the world, you never know peace."

Jimmy Young began fighting in 1969, mostly in his native Philadelphia. His first two fights of note were both losses, to Randy Neumann in 1972 and to Earnie Shavers in 1973. He then ran off a string of twelve wins, including a rematch with Earnie Shavers in 1974, and a ten-round decision in 1975 against Ron Lyle.

So the stage was set in Landover, Maryland, where Young would fight Ali at the Capital Center on April 30, 1976. Young entered the ring weighing 209, while Ali, the reigning heavyweight champ, came in undertrained and overweight— at 230. It was the most he ever weighed for a fight; Ali claimed it was from "eating too much pie."

The fight was notable for the appearance of several Washington bigwigs, including Ted Kennedy. It also turned out to be more of a contest than people thought it would be, which might explain why the house was less than full.

Young used an approach similar to the one Ali had used against Foreman—leaning his head back, outside the ring ropes to make it tough for Ali to hit him. Young's tactic even incurred a ten-count by the referee in the twelfth round, but he quickly pulled his head back in. Ken Norton, sitting at ringside with TV announcer Howard Cosell, said the fight was too close to call as it headed for the last of the scheduled fifteen rounds. Ali kept missing with his punches, while Young fought gamely, wearing Ali out and landing blows to the head. They were not strong enough to do more than earn him points, however, and when it was all over, Ali won on all three cards, although one side judge only gave the champ a two-point edge.

The crowd booed the decision, feeling that Young had outfought Ali in the final rounds, and fought well enough, overall, to deserve the title. Young fought for another fifteen years, but never got another chance to fight for the title. He had problems later in his life with drugs and money. He died in Philadelphia of a heart attack on February 20, 2005.

Ali and Young battle each other during the WBC and WBA heavyweight championship fight at the Capital Center on April 30, 1976 in Landover, Maryland.

RICHARD DUNN

Ali was next scheduled to fight Richard Dunn at the Olympiahalle, in Munich, Germany, on May 24, 1976. Dunn was a true heavyweight champion, holding the British, Commonwealth, and European belts, the latter one gained in his last fight against German Bernd August just one month earlier. It quickly became clear to Ali that if he was going to win this fight, the substandard training he underwent prior to his fight against Jimmy Young would not do.

Dunn, a Yorkshire southpaw who stood a towering six feet, four inches, was one of the few opponents Ali had to look up to. Dunn had fought and mostly beaten some of the best European fighters. One of his defeats, though, came at the hands of Jimmy Young; he lost to the American with an eighth-round TKO at London's World Sporting Club. He won his next seven fights, however, which qualified him to meet Ali in Germany.

Ali vowed that Dunn would not be facing the apathetic fighter of the Young bout, he would be facing the old Ali, the one who trained hard. He got himself back down to 220 and knew he was ready. But so was Dunn. Both fighters spent the first round and a half, taking each other's measure, especially Ali, who, despite his bouts

with Joe Frazier, still felt awkward fighting a left-handed boxer. By the end of the second round, he finally figured Dunn out, hitting the Brit with a flurry of punches. Meanwhile, Dunn was getting his own licks in and showing Ali that he could give as good as he got.

The fourth round changed everything. Ali knocked the British champion down three times with straight right-hand punches. Dunn kept getting up and coming back for more, though by the third knockdown, he began to show a wobble in his step. Even though Dunn was still game, his spirit was stronger than his body. After Ali floored him a second time in the fifth round, just a little over two minutes in, the referee stopped the fight. Ali clowned as the result was announced, spinning his right hand around like a windmill. After the fight, Ali donated his gloves to a British charity, which he had promised to do. Inside one glove Ali wrote "Round five."

Dunn fought Joe Bugner the following October and lost his titles, lost his next fight, then retired, maybe not as champion, but certainly as a hero to his fellow Yorkshiremen, who had never before had one of their own wear a major boxing crown.

British heavyweight champion
Richard Dunn meets Muhammad Ali
at Quaglino's gym before his match
against Germany's Bernd August.
Dunn's victory over the German fighter
earned him a bout with the Greatest.

ALI GOES HOLLYWOOD

"People like to be puzzled, so I puzzle them."

With his good looks and outgoing public persona, Ali was a natural subject for motion pictures. While a number of documentaries were made about him while he was still fighting, including the intriguing *A.K.A. Cassius Clay* (1970), a vast number of documentaries were made as retrospectives after his retirement, including the outstanding *When We Were Kings* (1996), the poignant *30 for 30: Muhammad and Larry* (2009), and *Facing Ali* (2009), a collection of interviews with his former adversaries.

Ali even starred as himself in the 1977 biographical film *The Greatest*, which also featured Ernest Borgnine as Angelo Dundee and Rahman Ali and Drew Bundini Brown as themselves. The tagline read: WINNER, LOSER, LOVER, LOUDMOUTH . . . THE MAN. Based on many reviews of the film, especially of Ali's performance, it was a good thing he never decided to quit his day job. Ali also appeared in the 1979 TV movie *Freedom Road* as Gideon Jackson.

It is interesting to note that the popular song, "The Greatest Love of All," was introduced on the film's sound track played by George Benson. It went on to become a huge hit for Whitney Houston.

A major studio biopic, *Ali,* was produced in 2001 and starred Will Smith. Although Ali and other family members complained about some aspects of the script, the overall essence Smith captured was very similar to the Cassius Clay of those early news clips. It helped that the studio hired a superstar to play a superstar. Both Smith and John Voight (playing Howard Cosell) were nominated for Oscars, although neither won. Jamie Foxx, who played Bundini Brown in the film would go on to win Best Actor in 2005 for the biopic *Ray*.

Movie poster advertises *Ali the Man, Ali the Fighter,* a 1974 documentary on the life and career of Ali.

Ali Ali Ali

THE INCREDIBLE MUHAMMAD ALI YOU'VE NEVER SEEN BEFORE!

ALI! The poet, the clown, the folk hero the People's Champion, **ALI! THE MAN BEHIND THE MYTH!**

ALI! Winning, losing, then winning, and winning. From Liston to Frazier to Foreman... **ALI! THE BIG MOUTH WITH THE BIG PUNCH!**

Ali the man

Ali the fighter

Featuring **RICHIE HAVENS** From KATSU PRODUCTION COMPANY, LTD. Directed by RICK BAXTER; Executive Producer SHINTARO KATSU **G** IN COLOR

With **JOE FRAZIER** and **BURT LANCASTER** A WILLIAM GREAVES PRODUCTION. Presented by PETERSEN CHARTWELL ATTRACTIONS **G** IN COLOR

QUALITY ENTERTAINMENT FROM Cin America Releases Inc.

Poster for *A.K.A. Cassius Clay.* This film was made during Ali's exile from boxing after his refusal to be inducted into the U.S. Army on religious grounds.

MUHAMMAD ALI / CASSIUS CLAY

FLOAT LIKE A BUTTERFLY
STING LIKE A BEE

A FILM BY WILLIAM KLEIN · A DELPIRE PRODUCTION

AN EVERGREEN FILM PRESENTED BY GROVE PRESS AND ALVIN FERLEGER · SCA

The 1969 documentary *Float Like a Butterfly, Sting Like a Bee* (originally called *Muhammad Ali, the Greatest*), is a full-blown portrait of the boxer in and out of the ring. Footage from this film appears in many later documentaries.

CHAPTER ELEVEN

AN HONORABLE DEFEAT

"I never thought of losing, but now that it's happened, the only thing is to do it right. That's my obligation to all the people who believe in me. We all have to take defeats in life."

After his grueling 1976 Yankee Stadium fight with Ken Norton, a clearly exhausted Ali can barely muster the energy to field questions from the media.

KEN NORTON, THIRD FIGHT

"Norton must fall! Norton must fall!"
—Muhammad Ali

Somehow Muhammad Ali could not stay clear of controversy, even when fighting an old, respected foe. He and Ken Norton were each one for two, and, just as with Frazier, there needed to be a rubber match to settle the rivalry once and for all. Alas, based on the resulting rematch, few scores were ever settled with so little certainty, no vindication was ever so shaky.

After losing to Ali in 1973, Norton had subsequently lost to world champ George Foreman in a rousing title fight in Venezuela—which included Foreman knocking down Norton three times. Norton then redeemed himself with seven straight wins, including a TKO over Jerry Quarry in the Garden for the NABF title.

Now, for the first time in their three encounters, Ali was the world champion, meaning the combined heavyweight titles were again on the line. Norton would certainly be focused on finally achieving that elusive goal.

When they met that night on September 28, 1976, at Yankee Stadium, Ali was determined to employ his revised style of fighting. He'd come to learn his stamina wouldn't hold up for fifteen rounds of dancing, so he had adopted a new defensive technique, using his height, reach, and still-decent reflexes to strike out, but keeping his arms up, and feinting back or using rope-a-dope when he was attacked. Still, it was never all business for the champ—once in the ring, he chanted "Norton must fall!" for the crowd, and did his cartoonish windmill-windup while facing Norton's corner.

Considering these boxers knew each other's rhythms so well after two previous matches, it's not surprising that they were tied on the scorecards at the end of fourteen rounds. In the final round, Ali came out dancing and jabbing actively at the start. But then near the final bell, Norton leapt into action, pummeling Ali with his fists. Fight fans can be pardoned for believing Ken had taken the final round. But Ali won, based on both the judges' and referee's scorecards. The unofficial scorecard for the bout from UPI favored Norton, 8–7, while AP was for Ali, 9–6. The fight ended up becoming the fifth-most disputed title match in boxing history according to *Boxing Monthly.* What's not arguable is that Ali took a lot of hits, and that his plan to keep Norton at bay had not succeeded.

Norton was crushed by the decision and stood in tears when Ali as was declared the winner. There is a story circulating that many years later, during a photo shoot featuring

"The two first fights were close, they could have gone either way, but I knew as soon as the bell rang I won the third fight."

—KEN NORTON

these legendary boxers, Ali leaned over and said to Norton, "That third fight, I think you got it, champ!"

Not long after the rematch, Ali temporarily retired from the ring, determined to spend his time spreading the message of Islam. Norton would be awarded the WBC title in 1977, when it was stripped from Leon Spinks for refusing a Norton fight in favor of an Ali rematch. Ken then lost it to Larry Holmes in his first title defense—deemed the tenth-best heavyweight fight of all time.

Ken Norton was inducted into the World Boxing Hall of Fame in 1989 and into the International Boxing Hall of Fame in 1992. He is also in the U.S. Marine Corps Sports Hall of Fame. The former fighter acted in numerous films and TV shows, as well as appearing the reality show *Superstars* in 1976. A car crash in 1986 left him with speech problems.

His son Ken Norton Jr. was a football star at UCLA and had a long career in the NFL. Another son, Keith, works in broadcasting as a sports anchor.

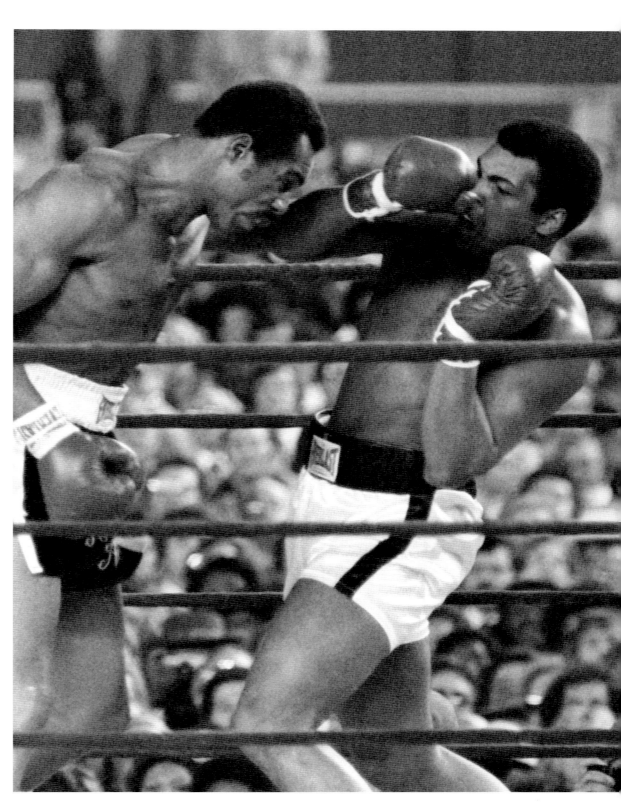

Ali leans back out of range as Norton closes in.

ALI, FAMILY MAN

Ali loved children, and they in turn were drawn to him wherever he traveled. He enjoyed spending time with his own brood and was often photographed at home with them. Once, when asked if he had any regrets, he answered that he was sorry he'd not gotten to spend more time with his kids when they were young and that he'd missed much of their childhoods, partially due to the demands of training and fighting but also as the result of divorce.

He has nine children in total. With second wife Khalilah, Ali had three daughters and a son: Maryum, twins Rasheda and Jamillah, and Muhammad Ali Jr. With third wife Veronica Porsche, he had two more daughters: Hana Yasmeen and Laila. Finally, Ali and his fourth wife, Lonnie, have an adopted son, Asaad Amin.

Two more daughters, Miya and Khaliah, whom Ali acknowledged, were from two extramarital affairs.

These girls were around the same age as Hana and Laila, and Hana recalls them all vacationing together at their father's ranch in Berrien Springs, Michigan. Hana added, "It was good because it wasn't some secret we discovered later in life."

Ali looked after his children financially while they were young, even after his relationships with their mothers ended. Once they were grown, however, he expected them to find their own way in the world. While the older Ali siblings are currently living productive, adult lives, Muhammad Jr. has struggled to find his footing.

MARYUM ALI

Maryum "May May" Ali became a hip-hop singer who leaned toward uplifting lyrics. While composing her own songs, she realized she enjoyed writing. She now works on screenplays and television concepts and also wrote a children's book about her famous father called *I Shook Up the World: The Incredible Life of Muhammad Ali*. Maryum holds a degree in social work and was part of LA Bridges, a delinquency prevention program. She is also deeply involved, as are her siblings, in raising Parkinson's awareness.

JAMILLAH ALI

In 2010, Jamillah married Michael Joyce—a Chicago lawyer who promotes young boxers—in Naples, Florida. Joyce, the son of former Illinois State Senator Jeremiah Joyce, was himself a prizefighter under the name "Irish Mike Joyce."

RASHEDA ALI

Rasheda works as a writer and speaker. Inspired by her father's battle with Parkinson's and after observing the way her children interacted with him, she wrote *I'll Hold Your Hand So You Won't Fall: A Child's Guide to Parkinson's Disease*. She wanted a book that would answer a child's questions about the disease as it progressed, something she and her siblings never had. She is also an advocate of stem-cell research and travels the world to speak on the effects of Parkinson's.

Ali in 1973 with his three eldest daughters, Maryum, Jamillah, and Rasheda. The girls' mother,, Khalilah Ali also gave birth to his eldest son, Muhammad Ali Jr.

MUHAMMAD ALI JR.

The boxer's first son is married and lives in Chicago. He has had a difficult time trying to move away from his father's long shadow: a rocky relationship with Lonnie Ali has not helped. Muhammad Jr. occasionally attends sports collectors' shows with celebrity promoter Howard Gosser to make public relations appearances and sign autographs.

HANA YASMEEN ALI

Hana Yasmeen became a writer and eventually helped her father pen his autobiography, *The Soul of a Butterfly: Reflections on Life's Journey*, which is an inspirational collection of anecdotes, spiritual reflections, and poems.

LAILA ALI

Laila, in spite of her father's protests, went on to become a professional boxer herself. (see Chapter Thirteen).

MIYA ALI

Miya Ali, one of Ali's acknowledged "love children," attends many Ali-related and boxing-related events, sometimes with her siblings. She was with her father when he met archrival Joe Frazier at the 2002 NBA All-star Game in Philadelphia and watched as the two men relaxed and shared laughs.

KHALIAH ALI

Khaliah Ali, one of Ali's two "love children," was born in 1974, when the fighter was still married to his second wife, Khalilah. The young woman is working on a memoir *Butterflies and Bees: A Woman's Search for Her Father*, which details her mother's life with Ali and her own sense of having been abandoned by him in later years.

She reveals that Ali was twenty-five and her mother, Wanda Bolton, was sixteen when they began their affair. Her mother, she says, was married to Ali 1975 in an Islamic ceremony conducted by Elijah Muhammad. Bolton then became Aaisha Ali, joined Ali's entourage, and eventually became friends with rival Khalilah.

ASAAD AMIN ALI

Ali's second son came to him like an unexpected blessing. Lonnie's sister was fostering the newborn for a friend until adoptive parents could be found, when Ali and Lonnie came for a visit. After Ali held the baby, the champ refused to go home without him. He and Lonnie formally adopted Asaad in 2006. The young man bears a surprising resemblance to Ali, with his wide smile and smooth complexion. He excelled at baseball as a boy and led his high school team to a division title in Niles, Michigan. In 2009, the Angels drafted him in the fortieth round, but young Ali preferred to go to college at Louisville University, where he became the team's catcher. In early 2012, the Florida Marlins came calling and were considering signing him.

ABOVE: Ali as doting dad, feeding his daughter Hana at a press conference before the London premiere of *The Greatest* in 1977.

BELOW: Ali cuddles with his daughters at Grosvenor House Hotel in London in 1978.

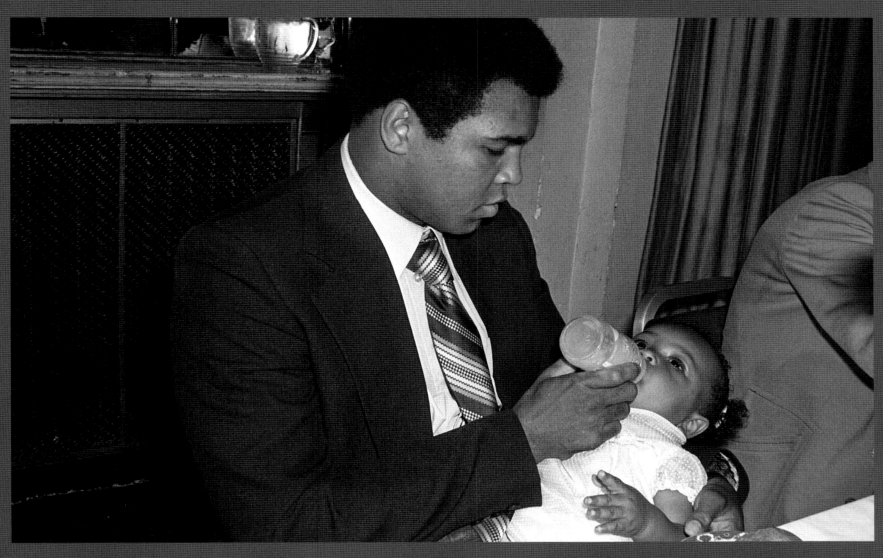

ALFREDO EVANGELISTA

"I'm thirty-five years old, and I danced fifteen rounds. It's a miracle."

Alfredo Evangelista fought Ali at the Capital Center in Landover, Maryland, on May 16, 1977. Ali had recently waltzed through two exhibition matches with Michael Dokes and Jody Ballard, and he predicted the bout with Evangelista would be about as challenging.

Evangelista was born in Uruguay, fought out of Spain, and was nicknamed the Lynx of Montevideo. He was the European heavyweight title-holder from 1977 to 1979, and as boxing tradition dictated, the EBU champ typically got a shot at the world champ. (This possibly also explains the travesty that was Coopman, who was ranked No. 1 in Europe at the time of his Ali fight) Still, Evangelista had a fairly decent record. This twenty-two-year-old workhorse had fought thirteen fights in fifteen months before he met Ali, with only one loss and one draw. Unfortunately the loss happened during the fight just prior to his bout with Ali; not exactly great for building confidence.

Ali came out dancing, and from the start, seemed to be toying with his opponent. Evangelista got some laughs from the crowd when he started dancing in time with Ali. At that point there was a lot of choreography going on and little pugilism, and when broadcaster Howard Cosell mentioned that Ali was grunting when he swung, he apologized and explained that there was nothing else to report other than "a Rogers and Astaire reprise." When the first round ended with little boxing action in evidence, Cosell called it a "vaudeville act."

But things finally heated up. Evangelista ended up surprising Ali throughout the middle of the fight, dominating the action in the seventh and eighth rounds. After the twelfth round, when Evangelista's youthful stamina refused to flag and he repeatedly tagged the champ, Ali appeared exhausted. He rallied in the thirteenth and nailed Evangelista with a strong right. The outcome was foregone by then; the fight went the full fifteen, and Ali would win by a unanimous decision. Cosell captured the essence of the fight when he called it "perfectly uneventful."

Evangelista later fought Larry Holmes for the WBC title, but lost to a seventh-round knockout.

Alfredo Evangelista tucks as Ali swings—some powerful action amid the dancing at the May 1977 title bout in Landover, Maryland.

EARNIE SHAVERS

Earnie Shavers was one of the hardest-hitting punchers to ever vie for the heavyweight title. So sayeth Larry Holmes, among others. And Shavers fought that way his whole career, with enormous reserves of power.

Shavers, who worked out in the Youngstown, Ohio, suburb of Warren, had been the 1969 National AAU heavyweight champion. As a pro, he soon acquired a record of 44-3 included 27 straight victories by KO. A majority of those fights didn't even go past the second round. He soon became known as the "Black Destroyer." But Shavers didn't really hit the big-time—in terms of money or brand-name opponents—until he chose a local promoter named Don King to be his manager.

Shavers's first victory of note was his first-round KO of Jimmy Ellis at Madison Square Garden in 1973. In another fight at the same venue, however, Shavers himself was knocked out in the first round by Jerry Quarry, who caught Shavers with a left, then pummeled him until the fight was stopped with barely two-and-a-half minutes gone. He also lost a unanimous ten-round decision a month earlier to journeyman Bob Stallings, in a fight that took place at the Felt Forum, next door to the Garden. And during a ten-round match fought in Denver, Shavers was knocked down by Ron Lyle, who defeated him with a sixth-round TKO.

Perhaps this inability to take a punch is what kept Shavers from fighting in a title match until he was thirty-two. But, having finally gotten there—with a scheduled bout against Ali in the offing—Shavers was determined to make the most of his chance. It wouldn't be easy, though, going up against an Ali who was reinvigorated after having beaten such worthy opponents as Richard Dunn and Ken Norton. Before the fight, Ali began with his taunting, calling Shavers the "Acorn," because of his smoothly shaved head.

The match took place at Madison Square Garden on June 29, 1977, and went the full fifteen rounds. It was a classic brawl between two pros. There were no knockdowns, but not from any lack of trying. Shavers left his glass jaw in the locker room, and managed to last the full fifteen, in part, because age was now becoming a factor with Ali. He might have taken out Shavers when he was in his prime, and he did daze his opponent late in the fight with some solid rights. But his speed and strength were not the same, plus he left his guard down often enough for Shavers to get in several shots that staggered the champ, though Ali's ability to shake off direct hits was still in evidence.

The Garden crowd cheered both opponents, knowing that they were witnessing a classic match-up between a legendary champion and a top-notch contender. When it was over, Shavers had lost on all three judges' cards, but he'd sure let Ali know that he had been in an honest to goodness fight. Ali himself said that Earnie "shook my kinfolk back in Africa" with his hard punches.

Shavers kept fighting until he was over forty, amassing a 74-14-1 record, including sixty-eight knockouts. *The Ring* magazine named him the tenth-greatest puncher of all time.

Shaver's hard-hitting right connects with Ali's jaw during the fight at New York's Madison Square Garden.

THE WIT OF ALI

"Boxing is a lot of white men watching two black men beat each other up."

"I'll beat him so bad he'll need a shoehorn to put his hat on."

"My toughest fight was with my first wife."

—REFERRING TO SONJI,
WHO REFUSED TO CONVERT TO ISLAM

"I told them, 'Get in the back—it'll be like *Driving Miss Daisy.*'"

—ALI ON GIVING RIDES
IN HIS CAR TO WHITE ASSOCIATES

LEON SPINKS

Leon Spinks was the most unlikely heavyweight champion to ever don gloves and trunks. After only seven professional fights, St. Louis native Spinks actually got to step into the ring with Muhammad Ali on February 15, 1978, at the Las Vegan Hilton.

Spinks had an impressive amateur record—AAU Light-Heavyweight Champion from 1974 to 1976 and Light-Heavyweight Gold Medalist at the 1976 Olympic games in Montreal. Then, as a pro, he'd stepped up into the heavyweight division and won his first five fights by KO. After a draw and two more victories by decision, including a win over undefeated Italian boxer Alfio Righetti, Spinks got to fight for the title.

A younger Ali once said that he would like to go on a NASA spaceflight to Mars to find an opponent, "'Cos there ain't no competition down here." He must have had that same thought while training for his bout with Spinks, whom he believed would offer him little challenge. Ali's weight had gone up to 224 pounds, but he wasn't that concerned; he had gotten away with the extra poundage against Jimmy Young (though the fans at that bout thought otherwise). But Spinks was more than a decade younger than

Ali, and more fit than the champ. He was therefore deserving of more respect, which he did not get. And the lack of training, for the first time, would prove costly to Ali.

Ali was at least honest with himself over how much his punching power had diminished. He was no longer able to weaken opponents with his legendary left jab, and then use the stinging right to drop them. This meant he often had to go the full fifteen rounds—which this fight did.

As the bout went on and on, Ali clearly showed sign of fatigue. Although Ali was still able to take a punch like no one else, Spinks managed to connect with enough blows to score points with the judges, even without doing any real damage. And when the fight ended, Spinks's glove-work had earned him a shocking split decision over Ali. The challenger was now the undisputed heavyweight champion.

Ali was in shock. But the loss was largely his fault. He knew he was no longer the fighter he'd once been, yet he hadn't even given himself an edge by slimming down. Plus, for the first time he hadn't been able to win over the judges with his usual charm and guile.

The inexperienced Leon Spinks seems as surprised as delighted at his upset win over Ali in a fifteen-round split decision.

SPINKS REMATCH

"They're selling video cassettes of the Ali-Spinks re-match for $89.95. Hell, for that money Leon will come to your house."

—DR. FERDIE PACHECO

Leon Spinks's unified title was split in two as soon as his reps announced that he would fight Ali in this rematch. The WBC's number-one contender was Ken Norton, and when he wasn't chosen as Spinks' next opponent, they stripped Spinks of his WBC crown. This would have great consequences down the road for Ali, as it turned out. The former champ, looking to get even, got himself back into shape, claiming he'd worked harder than he ever had to prepare for a fight, and with good reason—Muhammad Ali had announced earlier that this fight would be his last.

As the September 15, 1978, rematch approached, Ali decided there would be no clowning on his part, no mugging. He was determined to win it, and used all his available energy to achieve that goal. Again, the fight went the full fifteen rounds, in front of a record 63,000 energized fans at the Louisiana Superdome in New Orleans.

Spinks tried to take the fight to Ali as he had done in the previous bout, but Ali was more like his old boxing self, shuffling and eluding his opponent, making it difficult for Spinks to hit him effectively. And by the end of the fight, Ali's experience, determination, and talent won out over youth and ability, and judges and refs awarded him in a unanimous decision. Ali had helped himself by winning the later rounds and showing little evidence of flagging, all to put this fight in the winning column . . . thus making him the only three-time world heavyweight champion.

There was one fly in the ointment, however: Ali had gained only the WBA heavyweight title. The WBC title, which had been taken away from Spinks—for fighting Ali again instead of top contender Ken Norton—had gone to Norton, who then lost it to Larry Holmes when he defeated Norton in a fifteen-round split-decision at Caesar's Palace just three months earlier.

Ali retired after the Spinks rematch, but the fact that the WBA crown was not in his possession did not sit well with him. He wasn't happy with a non-unified belt; he wanted it all, and it would prey on his mind for the next two years. Meanwhile, Holmes, still the titleholder, kept racking up more victories, seven in total since he beat Norton.

Ironically, Spinks would twice win back the WBC title after Ali retired (but not the unified title that Ali desired) finally retiring in 1995 with a record of 26-17-3.

Sadly, Spinks suffers from pugilistic dementia, and has had many jobs in many places since his fighting days ended.

Determined to walk away the victor, Ali aims a short left hook at Leon Spinks during the rematch of title bouts at the Louisiana Superdome in New Orleans.

LARRY HOLMES: THE LAST HURRAH

"It was the money," said Wali Muhammad, Ali's assistant trainer, in the film Muhammad and Larry, explaining how the thirty-eight-year-old, overweight, out-of-shape boxer had been induced to come out of retirement to fight strapping new heavyweight champ, Larry Holmes. Sure, $8 million was a considerable lure, but there was also a title belt up for grabs, one that Ali wanted.

Larry Holmes, the "Easton Assassin," grew up poor in Pennsylvania and performed a series of menial jobs before taking up boxing at age nineteen. After accumulating an impressive amateur record of 19-3, he turned pro in 1973. Much of his early training came from the stellar boxers he worked for as a sparring partner— Muhammad Ali, Joe Frazier, Earnie Shavers, and Jimmy Young.

As a pro, he posted an astonishing series of wins, 35-0, and when he bested Shavers in 1978, it set Holmes up for a shot at WBC champ Ken Norton. That highly competitive fight went to Holmes in a split decision. He was now the bearer of the WBC title, the one title Ali craved. And so Ali came out of retirement to battle Holmes in an outdoor arena at Caesar's Palace on October 2, 1980. He was determined to take the cash, win the belt, and become the first four-time world heavyweight champion.

Ali came out of retirement to fight Larry Holmes, but he can't come out of his corner after his defeat against the then current champion.

Prior to the match, the Nevada State Athletic Commission (responding to media fears that Ali was unwell) ordered the fighter to undergo a physical. Ali was not happy, but he decided that if he had to go, he would go to the best medical facility in the United States, the Mayo Clinic. The doctors found little wrong with him physically. Ring doctor Ferdie Pacheco had noted his suspicions that Ali might have sustained some kidney damage, but they found none. What they did find was perhaps more disturbing.

During Ali's neurological exam a CAT scan of his brain showed a small hole in the membrane separating the ventricles. This was probably a congenital defect, the doctors told the boxer, and not the result of head trauma. What no one explained, however, was if it could be made worse by repeated blows. Ali also exhibited difficulty in speaking—caused by a lack of coordination of the muscles in the mouth, little agility when asked to hop, diminished motor skills, and a slight degree of miscalculation when asked to touch his finger to his nose.

In spite of these findings, which might have indicated early signs of brain damage, the doctors gave Ali a clean bill of health, and his license to fight was granted. Meanwhile, a British neurologist who had been studying film footage of Ali concluded that he was showing signs of brain damage. When Don King, who was promoting this fight with his own money, heard about this doctor's report, he told Ali to sue the man for trying to make a long-distance diagnosis. The fight would go on as scheduled. (Oddly, King did not back Ali, insisting he would "meet his Waterloo" in Holmes, and then adding, "This will be Ali's last hurrah.")

Ali worked incredibly hard to get back in shape at his Deer Lake camp, but there were other factors at work. He had started taking thyroid pills on the advice of Elijah Muhammad's doctor, but instead of following the recommended dosage, he was "popping them like vitamin tablets," with the result that he felt increasingly sluggish. Yet that didn't stop him from bragging of how he would beat Holmes, his good friend and former sparring partner.

In spite of Ali's boasts, once the fight began no one in his corner was surprised when Holmes immediately delivered a serious blow to the gut. The pummeling continued for round after round, with Ali barely able to get his gloves up to protect his face. It was pitiful to watch, as the once-brilliant fighter seemed to dodder from spot to spot in the ring. Was it the severe heat, the fans wondered, that had put Ali into such a stupor?

Holmes kept looking at the referee, expecting him to end the clearly mismatched fight. When there was no official intervention, Holmes bore down, hoping, he later explained, to mercifully end the fight with a KO. But Ali simply would not go down. Angelo, for once heedful of Ali's wishes, refused to yank his fighter, even though pleas for a swift resolution were audible in the crowd. Toward the end of the tenth round, Holmes, seeing Ali had nothing left, began pulling his punches.

Ring legend insists that Ali's manager, Herbert Muhammad—the son of Elijah Muhammad—was so distressed over his fighter's plight that he sent word from his seat that the bout must end, that Ali must admit defeat. Finally, just before the eleventh round, Ali's team threw in the towel, Angelo declaring, "The ball game's over." The announcers, sportswriters, and fans that had bemoaned the carnage, all breathed a sigh of relief.

The Ali who slumped from the ring in Las Vegas would pay heavily in the years to come for the damage he sustained that night; replays of the fight would show he took more than 125 hits in the ninth and tenth rounds alone.

Larry Holmes wept openly at the end.

Holmes comes on strong during Ali's penultimate match, which took place outdoors in the Caesar's Palace parking lot.

"Muhammad could take a very good punch. He was slick, he could move, he could hit, make you miss, good hand speed and combinations and one of the greatest fighters of all time in my opinion."

—LARRY HOLMES

TREVOR BERBICK, DRAMA IN BAHAMA

If it was at all possible, Ali was going to redeem himself in this, his final fight. After the endless, painful somnambulism of the Holmes match, it seemed doubtful that he would have the wherewithal to ever step into a ring again. But after a year off, he appeared refreshed and restored—if somewhat overweight—a beefy new version of the former champion.

When Ali decided he wanted one more fight before retiring, it hadn't been easy to find an opponent or a venue. Several boxing commissions, concerned about his questionable health and disintegrating skills, were leery of giving him permission to fight. It was Nassau, in the Bahamas, that ultimately hosted the match, and Trevor Berbick, the relatively unseasoned Canadian champ, who was chosen to meet him.

Berbick was a Canadian-Jamaican fighter who had represented Jamaica in the 1976 Montreal Olympics, falling to Romanian silver medalist Mircea Simon. He liked Canada enough to settle there, boxing out of Montreal and Halifax. In 1979 he won the Canadian heavyweight title—vacated by the retiring George Chuvalo—by defeating Earl McLeay.

Before the fight, Ali was bragging again as he jogged across Paradise Island—"I'm like I was in Manila. I'm movin' and punchin' now like in Manila . . . Ten rounds is so simple. I can sizzle and dance for ten rounds. This man stands still and waits . . . Berbick's easy to hit. He's so easy to hit that he gets mad if you miss him."

The fight was held on December 11, 1981, but it nearly didn't take place. Berbick wanted his full $350,000 fee up front and while the promoters scrambled to find the money on the day of the bout, Berbick refused to leave his room. (The promoters had also neglected to supply enough boxing gloves, and there was a request made during the undercard matches not to cut the glove's laces at the end of a fight.)

From the very start of the fight, Ali came out on the attack. In spite of weighing in at 236, his heaviest fight weight ever, he appeared to be in very good condition. The announcers were impressed, remarking that they were seeing more action in this first round than in all of the Ali-Holmes fight. Berbick began forcing Ali onto the ropes, and then managed to score some strategic shots to Ali's midsection.

Berbick and Ali battle it out at the Queen Elizabeth Sports Centre in Nassau, the Bahamas. Berbick took the fight in a ten-round unanimous decision.

"Boxing was nothing. It wasn't important at all. Boxing was just a means to introduce me to the world."
—MUHAMMAD ALI, 1983

During the early rounds the two men kept to the same routine, Ali jabbing for the head, Berbick going for the body, Ali on the ropes, then clinching Berbick tight and being pulled off by the ref. In the fourth round, Ali took serious hits to the head and body, but rallied near the end with impressive force. Berbick came out strong in the fifth, which ended with a slugfest between the two fighters. In the sixth round, Berbick appeared to be tiring, and both men began boxing cautiously. The seventh found Ali on the ropes again, and Berbick all over him with calculated body blows.

The crowd cheered when Muhammad came out dancing and jabbing in the eighth, crying "Ali, Ali!" But the dancing stopped when Berbick tagged him hard on the face. Ali danced again in the ninth, but his trusty left jab was now weakening and ineffective. Ali fell back to the ropes, trying to hold off Berbick, but getting hit all the same. At least that much hadn't changed—he could still take punishment better than any fighter.

During the final round, Ali looked tired, but he and Berbick were both dancing. Ali fought on gamely, but near the end, Berbick got in some good punches.

At the end of the tenth round, many people in the crowd—and those in Ali's corner—believed he had won the fight. But the match ultimately went to Berbick in a unanimous decision. Ali was naturally disappointed, trying to stay philosophical.

Yet this outcome was certainly not another bitter pill, not on the scale of the Holmes embarrassment, as Ali (and his fans) must have feared. Instead of annihilation, Ali found some measure of vindication. No, it wasn't a fight for the ages, far from it. But he had proven he was not a broken-down, aging palooka, but a warrior who still occasionally carried lightning in his gloves. Not an unfitting finale for one of the world's greatest and most talented fighters.

Ali, famous for his ability to take punishment, battled bravely during his ten rounds with Berbick.

CHAPTER TWELVE

THE LION IN WINTER

"There are more pleasant things to do than beat up people."

Muhammad Ali takes a well-earned rest in a London park on the morning after his victory over Henry Cooper in May 1966.

A BUSY RETIREMENT

"No matter what God gives you, you have to stand up to this test. There's a reason. There's a reason that the Parkinson's has affected his voice. It doesn't affect everybody's voice who gets Parkinson's. Maybe it was to sort of quiet him down."

—Lonnie Ali

Ali officially retired in 1981, but it was not his fate to drift off into those relaxed and restful golden years most people dream of.

For one thing there was more marital discord to deal with. He and Veronica had been drifting apart for some time, and now she expressed interest in modeling in Paris. Ali, who had begun to show signs of neurological impairment, was already in a supportive relationship with his old friend from Louisville, Yolanda "Lonnie" Williams. She continued to look after his health in Los Angeles, while he sorted out his marriage. Once he and Veronica officially split in 1986, Ali was free to marry Lonnie.

Lonnie, a former Kraft Food sales rep with an interest in brand management, had just received her business masters degree from UCLA. She set to work straightening out the tangled financial affairs of her new husband and created a corporation called G.O.A.T. (Greatest of All Time) to oversee his contracts, copyrights, and other legal obligations.

After a short time of looking into these business matters, she began to understand that he was much more than a boxer. Ali was a global brand, and as such needed to be treated as one. It became her task to choose the right commercial outlets for him (no alcohol, tobacco or gambling ads, for instance, due to his Muslim beliefs) and to make sure the things he now stood for in the public eye, his values and integrity, were never compromised.

On a side note, in April 2009, Lonnie Ali was among ten people named by President Barack Obama to the Presidential Commission for the Study of Bioethical Issues. This commission, according to the White House, will advise the president on bioethical issues that might emerge from advances in biomedicine and related areas of science and technology.

THE CHAMP FACES A NEW CHALLENGE

After Ali retired, there seemed to be increasing problems with his speech and his coordination. Finally, in 1984, Ali was diagnosed with Parkinson's syndrome, a condition that results in body tremors, slurred speech, limb rigidity, facial immobility, and other neurological problems. This syndrome, which is closely related to Parkinson's disease, is often seen in boxers and can be brought on by repeated blows to the face and head.

Ali told interviewers he first noticed something odd when initially his little finger began shaking and then his whole hand started shaking. He told himself that he had to fight this ailment, that he had to, "Knock it out."

Although many fight fans blamed boxing past his prime, and in particular the brutal Holmes fight, as the cause of his condition, Ali himself maintains the Parkinson's syndrome did not come from getting beat up in the ring. He likes to point out that all the fighters who got roughed up who do not have any signs of Parkinson's.

One of Ali's physicians, Dr. Mahlon DeLong, chair of neurology at Emory University in Atlanta, is convinced that Ali has full-fledged Parkinson's disease—just like a million other non-boxing Americans—and he bases this belief on how Ali's symptoms respond to medication.

Ali was prescribed Artane, which helps with tremor and muscular stiffness, and levodopa, a replacement for dopamine, the neurotransmitter missing in Parkinson's disease sufferers. Dr. DeLong, who believes Ali's condition is unrelated to boxing, feels Ali should have a normal life span providing he stays current with the newest medications and improved treatments.

Ali relaxes with a hot drink in Dublin, 1972.

REFUSING TO SLOW DOWN

"It wasn't the boxing, it was the autographs."
—ALI IN 2003

After his retirement in 1981, Ali was again a popular choice as a public speaker at conferences, conventions and college campuses, just as he had been during his exile from boxing. Even though the progressive symptoms of Parkinson's would increasingly hamper him in the 1990s, he was still actively sought after during that time, especially after his surprise appearance at the 1996 Atlanta Olympics when he lit the flame. Dozens of phone calls and hundreds of offers to appear or speak flooded his business offices. He found himself more in demand than ever for live appearances at sports cons, and for commercial endorsements, signed memorabilia, and autographs. He even did a famous "Got Milk" magazine advertisement in 2001 with daughter, and fellow pugilist, Laila Ali.

Ali also traveled the country promoting his books. In 1996 he and author Thomas Hauser toured high schools talking about *Healing*, Ali's inspirational counterpunch against bigotry. Later, he and daughter Hana together promoted his 2004 autobiography, *Soul of a Butterfly*, which she helped him write.

Even though Ali—who had won fifty-six fights and lost five— retired with lifetime earnings of $49 million, his various financial demands, taxes, divorce settlements, lawyer's fee, donations to the Nation of Islam, and entourage expenses left him with less that $4 million. So even though he devoted much of his post-retirement time to fund-raising, not all his engagements were for charity.

When he did receive in a fee, Ali was capable of earning upwards of $200,000 for a high-profile personal appearance. Lonnie, who handled his engagement calendar along with certain friends and advisers, would schedule speaking gigs up to fifteen or twenty times a year, depending on his health concerns.

Ali the Fighter, to paraphrase an old complaint from his past, had truly evolved into Ali the Event. He was soon making a very comfortable living from public appearances, merchandising, and endorsements.

Muhammad Ali autographs books at the ABA Convention in May 1994 in Anaheim, California.

INTERNATIONAL BOXING HALL OF FAME

"He's the only man I know where the kids come to the gate and say 'Can Muhammad come out and play?'"—

—KIM FORBURGER, ALI'S ASSISTANT

It seemed a foregone conclusion that Ali— the Greatest—would be inducted in to the International Boxing Hall of Fame. Still, any such recognition is sure to stir all but the most jaded hearts, and so in 1990 with great pride Ali attended the induction ceremony—and got to mingle with some of his own personal heroes.

The Hall of Fame is located in Canastota, New York, not far from two others sports meccas, the Baseball Hall of Fame in Cooperstown and the Soccer Hall of Fame in Oneonta. The first Boxing Hall of Fame was inside Madison Square Garden, but in 1990 it was moved to Canastota—home to champions Carmen Basilio and his nephew Billy Backus—after an initiative by Ed Brophy to honor this upstate town with its strong boxing legacy.

Ali was among the boxers, both present-day and from the past, who were inducted into the brand-new facility. Other 1990 Hall of Famers include: Jake LaMotta, Ike Williams, Sandy Saddler, Sugar Ray Robinson, Willie Pep, Jose Napoles, Archie Moore, Carlos Monzon, Rocky Marciano, Joe Louis, Henry Armstrong, Carmen Basilio, Ezzard Charles, Billy Conn, Bob Foster, Joe Frazier, Kid Gavilan, and Emile Griffith, plus a host of old-timers, including James J. Corbett, Jack Dempsey, Jack Johnson, Gene Tunney, and such ring pioneers as John L. Sullivan and Daniel Mendoza.

Traditionally a professional fighter must wait five years after retiring before he or she can be eligible for nomination. Each year the ceremony attracts not only the inductees, but also former boxing champions, and sports and entertainment celebrities.

Ali had already been inducted into the World Boxing Hall of Fame, in Riverside, California, on November 6, 1986.

Ali was inducted into the International Boxing Hall of Fame in 1990 along with other boxing legends, such as Archie Moore, Sugar Ray Robinson, Joe Louis, and Rocky Marciano.

MUHAMMAD ALI PARKINSON CENTER

The Muhammad Ali Parkinson Center Movement Disorders Clinic of Barrow Neurological Institute, part of St. Joseph's Hospital and Medical Center in Phoenix, Arizona, opened its doors in 1997. The facility was created with the intent of offering patients multiple services, instead of requiring them to visit separate locations. This integrated-care philosophy is especially critical for patients with movement disorders—like those with Parkinson's—who have trouble getting around.

The Center, established by Muhammad Ali, Phoenix philanthropist Jimmy Walker, and Dr. Abraham Lieberman, is dedicated to providing outstanding levels of diagnosis, treatment therapy, research, and education for people with Parkinson's disease, as well as those with other movement disorders.

Late in 2009, Ali made a rare public appearance with Lonnie to attend the opening of the newly expanded Parkinson Center in Phoenix. The original Center had space to treat maybe sixty patients a year, while the new center can treat up to 1,600 annually. This facility is now considered the most comprehensive in America for the treatment of this disorder, which typically causes tremors, halting movement, balance problems, and muffled speech. The Center's varied outreach programs include support groups, conferences, educational classes, research studies, assistance and recreational programs, and other necessary services.

At the time of their visit, Ali and Lonnie had become Phoenix residents, living in the suburb of Paradise Valley. After cutting the red ribbon with a giant pair of scissors, Ali, Lonnie, and her sister toured the facility, the two women holding Ali's hands. They stopped occasionally to admire the framed photos from the former heavyweight champ's boxing career that line the hallways.

Ali himself has again become a metaphor for grace under pressure, this time as an example of how to cope with a debilitating disease with dignity and humor. His example is especially meaningful to other Parkinson's sufferers. As Dr. Leiberman says, "I tell patients, 'Look, Muhammad Ali was the greatest athlete in the twentieth century. He's got Parkinson's and he's not desperate, he's not dejected, he's not depressed.'" He adds, "The Center is named for him because he's such a recognizable figure, and he's given so much inspiration to people."

Ali and his wife, Lonnie, cut the ribbon to dedicate the Muhammad Ali Parkinson Center at Barrow Neurological Center in Phoenix, Arizona, on December 3, 2009.

CHAPTER THIRTEEN

THE LEGACY

"We have one life; it soon will be past; what we do for God is all that will last."

Ali's legacy stretches far beyond his achievements in boxing—he is also a sometime philosopher, poet, wit, philanthropist, spiritual leader, and spokesman for a generation. He was awarded the Presidential Medal of Freedom, he traveled to Iraq to negotiate directly with Saddam Hussein for the release of American hostages, and his appearances have raised millions of dollars in charitable donations.

HUMANITARIAN ACTS

"The service you do for others is the rent you pay for the time you spend on earth."

Over time, the effects of Parkinson's reduced the once-agile, lightning-fast, silver-tongued champion to a prisoner of the shaking limb, the shuffling gait and the mumbled sentence. Yet Ali did not let his physical deterioration keep him from the public eye. He used his fame to become a spokesperson for Parkinson's, raising money for research and increasing public awareness of the syndrome and other similar movement disorders.

In addition, he raised money for UNICEF, food relief for the hungry, the fight to end youth and gang violence, and the Special Olympics. Ali advocated for boxers and the improvement of the conditions in which they compete and was the sponsor of a successful 2002 congressional bill that addressed these concerns.

There have also been humanitarian missions Ali embarked on anonymously. Before the Gulf War began, in 1990, Ali flew to Iraq and met with Saddam Hussein to help negotiate the release of fifteen hostages. In 1997, he spoke out against the genocide and atrocities that were taking place in Rwanda, and then called upon Americans to support any charities that were helping these victims and their families.

More recently, Muhammad and Lonnie Ali have focused on social philanthropy, especially through the Muhammad Ali Center and the Michael J. Fox Foundation, which supports Parkinson's research. And in spite of his disability, Ali does occasionally appear in public; he toured Britain in August 2009, fund-raising and increasing awareness for his Alltech-Muhammad Ali Centre Global Education and Charitable Fund, and was part of the opening ceremonies at the 2012 London Olympics.

Joe Frazier, George Foreman, and Muhammad Ali—former ring rivals—team up for a 1989 charity event in London.

OLYMPIC TORCHBEARER

The climax of any Olympic ceremony is the lighting of the cauldron, the fire that will burn throughout the games and not be extinguished until the closing ceremony. The organizers of the 1996 summer games in Atlanta, Georgia, wanted a true American hero to carry the final stage of the torch's journey, and a former Olympic gold medalist, three-time heavyweight champion and United Nations "messenger of peace" was the man they chose.

Ali's inability to perform a run-through during rehearsal earlier in the day worried the organizers. They feared that he would be too weak to complete his task that evening, when 80,000 attendees and 3.5 billion viewers would be watching.

At the proper moment during that night's opening ceremony, as Beethoven's "Ode to Joy" filled the stadium, American distance swimmer Janet Evans lit her torch from the one jointly held by Atlanta-native boxer Evander Holyfield and Greek track-and-field star Voula Patoulidon. Evans started up the ramp toward the cauldron but near the top she paused as a figure emerged from the shadows. It was Muhammad Ali. The crowd gave a collective gasp and then roared its approval as the visibly shaking Ali held his torch to Evans's flame. Careful not to drop the torch, he moved gingerly to the cauldron's base and ignited a piece of fabric on a wire that then ascended to the cauldron, which burst into flame.

Bob Costas, covering the opening for NBC-TV, said, "Like everyone else in that stadium, I was deeply moved. Here's a guy who was once the most alive of men—the most dynamic and beautiful athlete we'd ever known—and now, to an extent, he was imprisoned by Parkinson's. His lighting that torch said something about the human spirit."

Later in the games, Ali was given a new gold medal to replace the medal he'd won in Rome during the 1960 summer games. As he tells it, he tossed that first medal into the Ohio River in disgust when he was refused service at a whites-only lunch counter in Louisville.

SUMMER LONDON OLYMPICS 2012

Ali was again part of the Olympics at London's 2012 Summer Games. Looking dapper but frail in a white suit and sunglasses, he stood beside Lonnie awaiting the procession that carried the outspread Olympic flag into the stadium. The eight flag-bearers approached Ali, and as the announcer presented him, Lonnie guided him right up to the flag's edge. Seconds later the flag-bearers moved on toward the center of the stadium, but then, like a tender afterthought, the final bearer—a young woman with upswept hair—gently touched Ali on his shoulder as she passed by.

Ali was seated during the rest of the ceremony, when seven promising young athletes lit the cauldron.

Muhammad Ali carries the torch to light the Olympic flame on July, 19, 1996, at the Olympic Stadium in Atlanta during the opening ceremony of the Centennial Olympic Games.

LAILA ALI, SHE BEE STINGIN'

"I'VE TRAINED HARDER, I'M BETTER,
I'M STRONGER, THE BLOOD OF A CHAMPION
RUNS THROUGH MY VEINS, I'VE EARNED
THIS OPPORTUNITY, I'LL EARN THIS VICTORY,
I'VE ALREADY WON."

When twenty-one–year-old boxer Laila Ali stepped into the ring on October 8, 1999, for her first pro match against another novice fighter, it should not have raised much interest among the press or the public. But this fighter was the daughter of the great Muhammad Ali, and so the world took notice, and a media crowd and three thousand people showed up for the bout in upstate New York.

As things turned out, it wasn't much of a contest. Ali, boxing as a super middleweight, beat her opponent, April Fowler, in the first thirty-one seconds of the match, not enough of a fight to earn bragging rights. Her second bout, however, ended only seconds from the final bell, and Ali had to work for her TKO victory against Shadina Pennybaker.

Laila was her father's second-youngest child, his second daughter with Veronica Porsche Ali. She'd started boxing recreationally at fifteen—but her news that she wanted to box in pro fights upset her dad. He warned her that women's bodies were not meant to take heavy blows. But had Laila been excited by the prospect ever since she was eighteen and had first learned that some women actually boxed as a career.

Ali finally accepted that his daughter was following in his footsteps, although he wasn't able to attend her most famous fight due to a prior commitment to NASCAR. Laila had won her next seven fights after Pennybaker, and her fans urged her to next fight either George Foreman's daughter Freeda or Joe Frazier's daughter, Jacqui Frazier-Lyde, who were both pro fighters.

On June 8, 2001, Laila and Jacqui met in a match the press called Ali/Frazier IV, riffing on the three fabled fights between their fathers. After going eight rounds, Laila won by a majority decision. It was the first time a prizefight headlined by two black women was broadcast on Pay-Per-View.

Laila took a year off for shoulder surgery and then bested Shirvelle Williams; Suzette Taylor —for the IBA title; Valerie Mahfood, for both the WIBA and IWBF belts; and Mary Ann Almager.

Laila Ali poses with her father after her ten-round WBC/WIBA Super Middleweight title bout with Erin Toughill at the MCI Center in Washington, D.C. Ali won the fight with a third-round TKO.

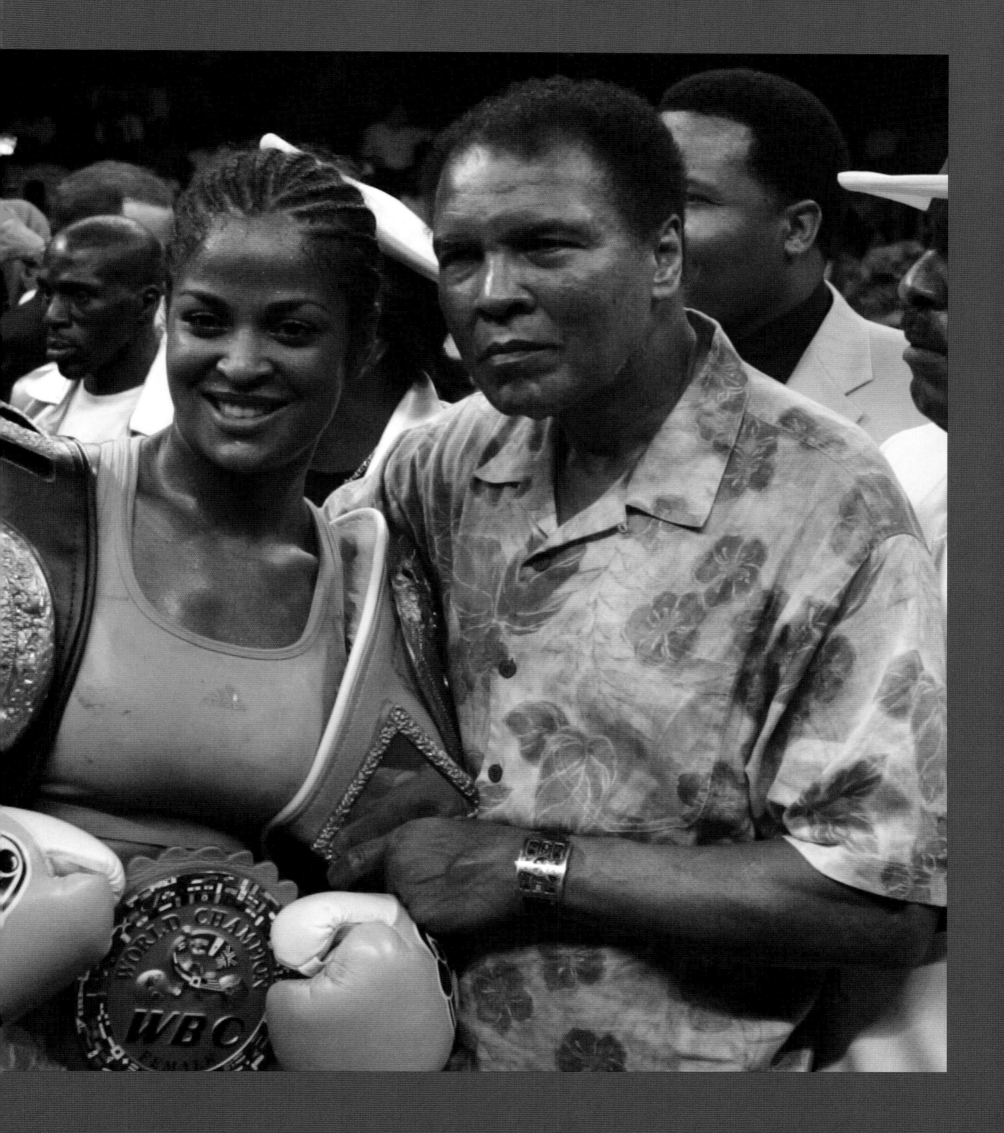

Ali, caption here

She again beat Mahfood in a June 2003 rematch, a slugfest that left Ali with a scar on her right eyelid. In August 2003 Ali knocked out Christy Martin, and in July 2004 she knocked out Nikki Eplion. Monica Nunez went nine rounds with her in Louisville before being TKOed. Laila then added the IWBF light heavyweight title to her resumé by knocking out Gwendolyn O'Neil in Atlanta.

It was also in Atlanta, in 2005, that Laila scored a decisive victory over Cassandra Giger with a TKO in the tenth. After fiercely beating Erin Toughill in three rounds, Laila gained the WBC title. (This fight is considered by many to be one of the most violent in women's boxing.) Ali was only the second woman to win a WBC title—after Jackie Nava. She traveled to Berlin to beat Asa Sandell with a disputed TKO, and then bested Shelley Burton in New York. What would become Laila Ali's final fight took place in 2007, Kempton Park, South Africa, where she fought a rematch with Gwendolyn O'Neil and again trounced her, this time in the first round. She retired an undefeated champion.

Boxing critics complain that Ali purposely avoided any stiff competition, other top female boxers who might have really tested her mettle. Anne Wolf, Vonda Ward, Leatitia Robinson, and Natascha Ragosina all claim they challenged her, but she always found a way to elude them.

Ali has been married twice, in 2000 to Johnny "Yahya" McClain, who became her manager, and in 2007 to former NFL player Curtis Conway. She has three stepchildren from her marriage to Conway: twins boys, Cameron and Kelton, and daugter, Leilani. She and Conway also had two children together, son Curtis Muhammad and daughter Sydney J.

In 2007 Ali was a contestant on the popular reality show *Dancing with the Stars*, where she was paired with fan-favorite Maksim Chmerkovskiy. She and Max danced well enough to make it to the finals, where they placed third, losing to Apolo Anton Ohno and Joey Fatone. Ali has also had a number of TV gigs, including co-hosting the revival of *American Gladiators* with Hulk Hogan. She presently co-hosts ABC-TV's *Everyday Health* on Saturday mornings.

Like other family members, Laila Ali spends time and energy supporting and raising money for her favorite causes, including the American Diabetes Foundation, the Kid's Café Program of Feeding America, A Place Called Home, Spirit of Women's Health Network, and the Milagro Foundation. And of course she is a frequent attendee of the annual Celebrity Fight Night, which raises money for the Muhammad Ali Parkinson Center in Phoenix.

Laila is the author, with David Ritz, of the 2002 title *Reach! Finding Strength, Spirit, and Personal Power*, wherein she discusses her early years, including her relationship with her father and time spent in jail. Laila was a troubled child, whose relationship with her father has not always been easy. She recalls feeling isolated a lot—often the plight of children of celebrity parents who sometimes focus on fame instead of family. Yet now that things are smoother between father and daughter, the Parkinson's has made it so hard for him to communicate. Most poignant for Laila is that she would like to discuss his past with him and cannot. "It is painful for me," she says, "because I would love to sit down and talk to my dad about the way he used to be when he was my age, when he was in his prime, because we are so much alike."

Laila Ali doesn't just follow in her father's shuffling footsteps inside the ring, she follows the example he set as a philanthropist. Here, she kicks off the Feeding America's Hunger-Free Families campaign at the Food Bank on September 28, 2010, in Pasadena, California.

PRESERVING THE LEGEND

"I am the greatest – I said that even before I knew I was."

After she wed Muhammad Ali, Lonnie used her keen business instincts to organize and gain some control over her husband's scattered and haphazard commercial empire. She soon realized, however, that preserving his legacy for upcoming generations was an equally important task. As vice-president of G.O.A.T.—the corporation she formed to handle all licensing and usage of Ali's intellectual property—she was in a position to ensure that the inspirational and motivational aspects of his life, plus the humanitarian and philanthropic work he and she accomplished together around the globe, would be elevated and preserved. (In 2006 the company was sold and renamed Muhammad Ali Enterprises.)

THE MUHAMMAD ALI CENTER

Perhaps the greatest impact she made toward that end was by being the driving force behind the Muhammad Ali Center in Louisville. This institution is dedicated to preserving his boxing history, his spiritual journey, and his position as spokesman of a generation, as well as making sure that his philanthropic and humanitarian work continues long after he is gone.

The Center opened on November 19, 2005, which happened to be Muhammad and Lonnie's 19th wedding anniversary. The $60 million non-profit is located in downtown Louisville, in what has come to be called Museum Row. Although the exhibits include many items of Ali boxing memorabilia, the center is also, at his request, a space for sharing ideas and beliefs and for promoting hope, respect and understanding. Both as a museum and as an educational forum, the Ali Center inspires children and adults to be as great as they can be by focusing on themes of peace, social responsibility, and personal growth.

Ali and his wife, Lonnie, receive rapturous applause on stage during the Grand Opening Gala for the Muhammad Ali Center at the Kentucky Center in Louisville on November 19, 2005. The Center is designed as a "global gathering place" to promote peace and tolerance and to inspire everyone to reach for his or her full potential.

CHAPTER FOURTEEN

ALI TODAY

"I wish people would love everybody else the way they love me. It would be a better world."

Ali today—still the fighter. Whether idolized or vilified, he meets all challenges with the same good spirit and good humor that he's always displayed.

THE ELDER STATESMAN

Ali is often referred to these days as an elder statesman, someone who, while not precisely in the political arena, has the international celebrity and worldwide respect to act as a campaign booster, diplomatic messenger, or hostage negotiator.

Back in 1976, Ali stumped for Jimmy Carter and other Democratic candidates, while in 2009 he attended the inauguration of Barack Obama, the first American president with a mixed racial heritage. In 1985 he stepped in to try to secure the release of four Americans who had been kidnapped in Lebanon. He flew on goodwill missions to Afghanistan and North Korea as an "ambassador for peace" for the United Nations, delivered more than one million dollars in medical aid to Cuba, and traveled to South Africa to meet Nelson Mandela after his release from prison.

This man, who was once such a divisive figure in America, now has the ability—sometimes by his very presence alone—to bring people together and to promote peace, understanding, and tolerance.

THE 2012 LIBERTY MEDAL

In September 2012, the National Constitution Center presented Muhammad Ali with the Liberty Medal during the celebration of the 225th anniversary of the United States Constitution. The Liberty Medal recognizes Ali as a champion of freedom who exemplifies everything the award was created to honor: individuals of courage and conviction who strive to secure the blessings of liberty to people around the globe.

This occasion marked Ali's second visit to the National Constitution Center; in 2003, at a special Flag Day ceremony just before the Center opened, Ali was the first to raise the American flag—which had flown in every state and U.S. territory—that hangs in the Great Hall Overlook.

Bill Clinton, who is the Chair of the National Constitution Center, explained the rightness of their choice: "It is very fitting that Muhammad Ali, a representative for the bicentennial of the Constitution, be awarded the prestigious Liberty Medal in 2012, as the nation celebrates the 225th anniversary of our founding document. Ali embodies the spirit of the Liberty Medal by embracing the ideals of the Constitution— freedom, self-governance, equality, and empowerment."

Ali after a news conference at the National Press Club in Washington, D.C, on May 24, 2011. Ali appealed to Iran's Supreme Leader for the release of U.S. hikers Shane Bauer and Josh Fattal, who had been detained in Iran since 2009.

A CONTINUING FAITH

"We all have the same god, we just serve him differently. Rivers, lakes, ponds, streams, oceans all have different names, but they all contain water. So do religions have different names, and they all contain truth."

So much of Muhammad Ali's world changed because he had the desire to investigate spiritual beliefs and religious outlooks beyond his own parochial Baptist upbringing. Yet in spite of all the conflict that the conversion to Islam brought to his life, he has never turned his back on the faith that first spoke to him so strongly all those years ago.

What has changed is that he has become more tolerant, especially when compared to that young Nation of Islam member who believed that the black race should keep separate from the white. As he amended in a 2005 interview with Oprah Winfrey, "Christians are my brothers, Hindus are my brothers, all of them are my brothers. We just think different and believe different."

Some of this new forbearance might be explained by Ali's conversion from the Nation of Islam to more mainstream Sunni Islam in 1975. Then in 2005 he became a devotee of Sufism, which is the inner, more mystic manifestation of the Islamic religion.

According to daughter Hana Yasmeen, he has "a collection of books by Hazrat Inayat Khan with Sufi teachings. He read them front to cover. They're old and yellow and torn. They're amazing. He always says they're the best books in the world." His faith is more spiritual these days, she says, than strictly religious, and adds that recently, due to health issues, he's had to forego the 5:00 a.m. prayer, a ritual he had kept to devoutly since becoming a Muslim.

He has also been involved in the distribution of Islamic educational materials and has helped to finance Islamic institutions, including the Masjid al-Faatir mosque in Chicago. He insists that "the truly great men of history want not to be great themselves but to help others and be close to God."

Ali has recently had to forego his 5:00 a.m. morning prayer ritual due to ill health, but his faith is still as strong as it ever was.

CELEBRITY FIGHT NIGHT

"With all of the prizes, trophies, awards, and treasures that my father has received and given away, his greatness lay in the way he kept the recordings of his children's voices protected in a small safe."

—HANA YASMEEN ALI, AFTER FINDING A LARGE CACHE OF TAPE RECORDINGS IN ALI'S HOME.

Celebrity Fight Night, which began in 1994, was the brainchild of philanthropist Jimmy Walker, who believed a celebrity fund-raising event would be a great way to raise money for local charities. The first fund-raiser featured the Phoenix Suns' Charles Barkley and Dan Majerle boxing with giant gloves; it was huge success. The following year a concert by Kenny Rogers added the extra gloss of live entertainment to the evening. Before long the event was featuring live music by major entertainers and attracting world-famous celebrities.

The Muhammad Ali Celebrity Fight Night Awards were added during the fifth year, to acknowledge sports figures, entertainers, and members of the business community who demonstrated the qualities associated with Ali and his quest to find a cure for Parkinson's. Past recipients of the award include Halle Berry, Jim Carrey, Billy Crystal, Robin Williams, Arnold Schwarzenegger, Larry King, Michael J. Fox, Donald Trump, Evander Holyfield, Tony Hawk, and a host of other luminaries.

On July 2, 2012, Dr. Abraham Lieberman of the Muhammad Ali Parkinson Center was handed a $3 million donation from Jimmy Walker representing Celebrity Fight Night, a gift that will allow even more expansion of the facility and its programs. Since the start of Celebrity Fight Night, the organization has contributed more than $22 million to the Center, but the 2012 check was the single-largest donation by far.

The Muhammad Ali Celebrity Fight Night Awards celebrate achievements that reflect the qualities associated with Ali.

"I'd like for them to say:
He took a few cups of love.
He took one tablespoon of patience,
One teaspoon of generosity,
One pint of kindness.
He took one quart of laughter,
One pinch of concern.
And then, he mixed willingness with happiness.
He added lots of faith,
And he stirred it up well.
Then he spread it over a span of a lifetime,
And he served it to each and every deserving
person he met."

—ALI FROM 1972 INTERVIEW WITH DAVID FROST

Muhammad Ali—truly the Greatest.

AWARDS

PROFESSIONAL ACHIEVEMENTS

- The first and only three-time lineal World Heavyweight Champion
- The first World Heavyweight Champion to come back from retirement and regain the title
- Won twenty-two World Heavyweight Championship fights and made 19 successful defenses

AWARDS AND RECOGNITION

- Named The Ring Fighter of the Year for 1963, 1972, 1974, 1975, and 1978
- Named Boxing Writers Association of America Fighter of the Year for 1965, 1974, and 1975
- Proclaimed "Fighter of the Decade" (1970s) by *The Ring* magazine
- Won the Boxing Writers' Association of America James J. Walker Memorial Award for 1984
- Inducted into the World Boxing Hall of Fame in 1986
- Inducted into the International Boxing Hall of Fame in 1990
- Named the greatest heavyweight of all-time by *The Ring* magazine in 1998
- Named the greatest heavyweight of the 20th century by the Associated Press
- Named "Athlete of the Century" by *GQ* magazine
- Named "Sportsman of the 20th Century" by *Sports Illustrated*
- Named "Sports Personality of the Century" by the BBC
- Inducted into the Florida Boxing Hall of Fame in 2010

DID YOU KNOW . . . ?

- Muhammad Ali is the brother of fellow boxer Rahman Ali, the father of female world champion Laila Ali, and the uncle of Ibn Ali.
- Ali graduated from Central High School in Louisville with a D- average, ranking 376 in a class of 391.
- Ali was afraid of flying after he had a rough flight going to California for the Olympic trials, so before he flew to Rome for the Olympics, he visited an army surplus store and purchased a parachute, which he wore throughout the flight to Rome.
- After returning to Louisville as the Olympic light heavyweight champion, Ali was refused service at a "whites only" restaurant. He was so disgusted that he threw his gold medal into the Ohio River.
- Ali's first fight with Joe Frazier indirectly led to four deaths:
  - Two spectators at Madison Square Garden died of heart attacks during the fight.
  - Erio Borghisiani was found dead in front of his television just hours after viewing the fight on paid television in Milan, Italy.
  - In Malaysia, Abdul Ghani Bachik was reported to have leaped up from his chair while watching the fight on paid television and shouted, "My God, Cassius Clay has fallen!" He then suffered a fatal heart attack.

HISTORICAL RANKINGS

- A *World Boxing* reader poll ranked Ali as the 5th-greatest heavyweight of all time in 1974.
- Historian Nat Loubet ranked Ali as the 9th-greatest heavyweight of all time in 1975.
- John Durant, author of *The Heavyweight Champions*, ranked Ali as the 4th-greatest heavyweight of all time in 1976.
- BBC Sports, former WBA president Bill Brennan, former *The Ring* editor-in-chief Nigel Collins, former *Boxing Illustrated* editor-in-chief Herbert G. Goldman, Showtime commentator Steve Farhood, and historian Arthur Harris all consider Ali to be the greatest heavyweight of all-time.

OTHER AWARDS:

- Presidential Medal of Freedom, 2005
- Liberty Medal, 2012
- Lifetime Achievement Award from Amnesty International

BIOGRAPHIES OF KEY FIGURES IN ALI'S LIFE

SONNY LISTON (C. 1930–1970)

There is no record of his birth and, although he used a date of 1932 for official purposes, it is thought that he was several years older than he claimed and probably didn't know in which year he was born. Born Charles Liston, in St. Francis County, Arkansas, he was the twenty-fourth child of a viciously abusive and alcoholic father. His mother left when he was around thirteen, taking some of her children but leaving Sonny. He ran away to St. Louis and turned to a life of crime. In June 1950, he was sentenced to five years in Missouri State Penitentiary; it was while he was in prison that he was encouraged to start boxing.

Liston fought fifty-four professional bouts with fifty wins (thirty-nine KOs) and four defeats (two KOs). He won the World Heavyweight title in spectacular fashion—beating Floyd Patterson and becoming the first man in boxing history to knock out a heavyweight champion in the first round. Ironically, he himself became the second heavyweight champion in history to be knocked out in the first round when he was defeated by Ali in 1965, having already lost his title to Ali in February 1963.

Liston died under mysterious circumstances, supposedly of a heroin overdose, although he had not previously been known as a substance abuser (besides being a heavy drinker) and his wife insisted that he had a phobia of needles. Conspiracy theories revolve around his well-documented, long-term association with the criminal underworld.

JOE FRAZIER (1944–2011)

Born in Beaufort, South Carolina, Joseph William Frazier was the youngest of eleven children in an impoverished farming family. From an early age he idolized Joe Louis and strived to emulate his hero—filling burlap bags with leaves and moss to practice his punches. At the age of fifteen, Frazier moved to New York to live with an older brother and, unable to find work, survived by stealing cars to sell to a Brooklyn junkyard.

Frazier moved to Philadelphia and found work at a slaughterhouse, where he famously continued his boxing practice by pounding sides of beef with his fists—inspiring the scene in the 1976 movie *Rocky*. He only took up boxing properly at seventeen, but his raw power caught the eye of trainer Yank Durham, under whose direction he won the gold medal at the Tokyo Olympics in 1964. He began his professional career in 1965 and beat such greats as Jerry Quarry, Oscar Bonavena, and George Chuvalo before being crowned champion in 1968.

Frazier's professional record was thirty-seven fights (twenty-seven KOs), four losses (three KOs) and one draw. He is most famous for three grueling battles with his nemesis, Ali, who had been stripped of his title before Frazier had had a chance to fight him. Ali insulted Frazier, repeatedly referring to him as a "gorilla" and an "Uncle Tom." Although Ali later expressed regret for such insults, Frazier harbored a lifelong resentment and after watching Ali, who was struggling with Parkinson's disease, light the Olympic torch in 1996 he could not resist telling reporters that he would have liked to have "pushed him in."

Following his retirement, Frazier enjoyed cameo appearances in a number of movies and appeared as himself in two *Simpsons* episodes. He ran his own gym in Philadelphia and continued to train young fighters until he was diagnosed with liver cancer in September 2011; he died just two months later. Ali attended his funeral and said: "I will always remember Joe with respect and admiration."

GEORGE FOREMAN (B. 1949)

Born in Marshall, Texas, George Edward Foreman was the fifth of seven children and was raised by his heavy-drinking stepfather, J. B. Foreman. His family moved to Houston, where he had a troubled youth as a notorious brawler among the local gangs. After dropping out of high school, he enrolled in the Job Corps. He was sent to Oregon where his supervisor, Doc Broadus, a keen boxing enthusiast, encouraged Foreman to channel his aggression in the boxing ring.

Famed as one of the biggest hitters in the history of boxing, Foreman was two-time World Heavyweight champion and had eighty-one professional fights: seventy-six wins (with an incredible sixty-eight KOs) and five losses (one KO). He retired from boxing following a loss to Jimmy Young in 1977 but made a remarkable comeback. In 1994, aged forty-five, he knocked out Michael Moorer to become the oldest heavyweight champion in history.

He finally retired from boxing in 1997 and went on to enjoy huge success as an entrepreneur, promoting the "Lean Mean Fat Reducing Grilling Machine." More than 100 million grills were sold worldwide and, in 1999, he sold the naming rights for $138 million. Foreman now lives with his fifth wife Mary Joan and has eleven children, including five sons called George: George Jr. and George III, IV, V, and VI.

GEORGE CHUVALO (B. 1937)

Born in Ontario, Canada, Chuvalo grew up in the Junction District of Toronto with his Bosnian parents and sister, Zora. Inspired by Joe Louis, he knew he wanted to be a boxer from an early age, joining a gym and having his first fight at the age of ten.

Chuvalo had ninety-three professional fights, with seventy-three wins (sixty-four KOs), eighteen losses (two KOs) and two draws. Known for his "cast-iron" chin, he was never knocked down in the ring and beat such greats as Doug Jones, Jerry Quarry, and Manuel Ramos. He was Canadian heavyweight champion for twenty-one years and, although he never won a world championship, he always insists that he beat Ernie Terrell in their 1965 title fight. Chuvalo complains that the referee was intimidated by "the mob," who allegedly supported Terrell, insisting that "Terrell couldn't hit me in the fanny with a bowl of sand."

After boxing, Chuvalo tried his hand in the movie industry without any real success. His personal life was marred by tragedy—he lost three sons to drug abuse and his wife to suicide following the death of their second son. George has a second wife, Joanne Chuvalo, and is stepfather to her two children, Jesse and Ruby. Together they tour high schools in Canada and the United States. talking about the dangers of drug abuse. Asked how he coped with such loss, he says, "I just stay on my feet." In 2011, a statue was erected in his honor in Sarajevo, in his parents' homeland of Bosnia and Herzegovina.

JERRY QUARRY (1945–1999)

Born in Bakersfield, California, into an Irish family of boxing enthusiasts—his father and two brothers were also professional boxers—Quarry received his first pair of gloves when he was just three years old. Trained by his father, he went on to win the National Golden Gloves Tournament in Kansas in 1964, knocking out all five opponents in three days.

He began his professional career in March 1965, and won fifty-three (thirty-two KOs) of his sixty-six bouts with nine losses (six KOs) and four draws, beating such greats as Floyd Patterson, Buster Mathis, and Earnie Shavers. He had title fights against Ellis, Frazier, Ali, and Norton but never managed to win, joking that he was "always the bridesmaid." Although very fast and tough, he cut easily and—weighing just 195 pounds at his peak—was relatively small compared to the majority of heavyweights.

Hugely popular, charismatic, and rich, he retired in 1975 following defeat to Ken Norton, and pursued a successful career acting and commentating. Yet he found it impossible to stay away from the boxing limelight, making a brief return to the ring in 1977, again in 1983, and finally—and disastrously—in 1992. By then he was suffering from dementia pugiistica—atrophy of the brain caused by repeated blows to the head—and had blown his $5 million fortune. Ultimately, he was incapable of feeding or dressing himself and was cared for by his brother James. Quarry died from cardiac arrest in January 1999.

KEN NORTON (B. 1943)

Kenneth Howard Norton was born in Jacksonville, Illinois. He was a superb all-around athlete and won a scholarship to Northeast Missouri State College for his skills in football, basketball, and track events. It was only when he enlisted in the Marine Corps that he was introduced to boxing, eventually winning three All-Marine Heavyweight titles.

Norton's professional career began at the age of twenty-three, following victory at the AAU Golden Gloves tournament in 1967. He had fifty fights with forty-two wins (thirty-three KOs), seven losses (four KOs), and one draw. Following a surprise defeat to Jose Luis Garcia in 1970, Norton read the motivational book *Think and Grow Rich* by Napoleon Hill, which he claims changed his life. He went on a fourteen-fight winning streak and made boxing history in 1973 when he challenged Ali for the NABF title and won, breaking Ali's jaw in the process. He lost two other closely contested title fights to Ali. He was awarded the WBC title in 1977 but lost his first defense in yet another epic battle, this time with the great Larry Holmes in 1978.

Norton retired when he was thirty-seven, but returned to the ring twice in the early 1980s. He pursued a successful career as an actor and commentator, appearing in around twenty movies. In 1986, Norton was in a car crash that left him with a fractured skull, jaw, and broken leg. Following his personal motto: "what the mind can conceive, the body can achieve," he made a remarkable recovery despite being told that he would never again walk or talk. He lives in Orange County, California, and is the devoted father of five children, including the football legend Ken Norton Jr., who was the first player to win a Super Bowl ring in three consecutive years.

OSCAR BONAVENA (1949–1976)

Oscar Natalia Bonavena was born in Buenos Aires, Argentina. He began boxing in 1958, at a local athletics club and left school early to pursue his boxing ambitions, working part time at a meat market to earn his keep. Having won several major tournaments in South America he moved to New York, under the management of World War II hero Marvin Goldberg.

Bonavena was just twenty-one years old when he debuted at Madison Square Garden. He beat Lou Hicks by a technical knockout in the first round and he quickly racked up a string of early knockouts. In a total of sixty-eight professional fights, he won fifty-eight (forty-four KOs), lost nine (one KO), and drew one. He beat such greats as George Chuvalo and was one of the few boxers ever to knock down Joe Frazier. He was knocked out only once in his entire career—by Ali in December 1970.

Although he could be charming and charismatic, Bonavena had a reputation for being a brawler in and out of the ring, as well as for being a heavy drinker and a womanizer. His shady dealings with brothel owner Jo Conforte and his wife, Sally (with whom Bonavena was allegedly having an affair), led to his rapid decline and untimely death. Following a series of disputes, Bonavena was shot dead by Conforte's bodyguard—the ex-convict Willard Ross Brymer—who was later charged with manslaughter. A statue has been erected in Bonavena's honor in Parque Patricios, Buenos Aires.

FLOYD PATTERSON (1935–2006)

Born in Waco, North Carolina, Patterson was the youngest of eleven children and experienced a wretched childhood. When his family moved to Brooklyn, New York, he was continually in trouble with the law and ended up in a reform school when he was just ten years old.

He started boxing when he was fourteen, trained by Cus D'Amato, and won the gold medal at the Helsinki Olympics as a middleweight in 1952. That same year he won the National Amateur Middleweight Championship and the New York Golden Gloves Middleweight Championship. As a professional, Patterson won the Light Heavyweight and Heavyweight world titles. With a total of sixty-four professional bouts, he won fifty-five (forty KOs), lost eight (five KOs), and drew one.

Patterson famously beat Archie Moore in 1956, winning by a knockout in five rounds to become the youngest World Heavyweight Champion in history—he was twenty-one years old. In 1959, he lost the title to Sweden's Ingemar Johansson but made boxing history again in 1960 by knocking out Ingemar in the fifth round of their rematch to become the first man ever to regain the Undisputed World Heavyweight Championship. Patterson beat many of the greats, including the powerful brawlers Bonavena and Chuvalo.

In retirement, he became chairman of the New York State Athletic and trained his adopted son, Tracy Harris Patterson, who won world titles in two weight divisions. In 1998 he was diagnosed with Alzheimer's and later contracted prostrate cancer. He died at home in New Paltz, New York, when he was seventy-one years old.

ARCHIE MOORE (1916–1998)

Born Archibald Lee Wright in Benoit, Mississippi, he had a troubled childhood and lived in a reformatory until he was eighteen years old. He began boxing in 1935 and had one of the longest professional careers in the history of the sport, spanning nearly thirty years and three major weight divisions. He also scored more knock outs than anyone in history and was stopped only seven times, despite the fact that he frequently ventured into the heavyweight division.

In an astonishing 219 professional bouts, Moore won 185 (131 KOs), lost 23 (7 KOs) and drew 10. His reputation was such that major contenders avoided matches with him, and it wasn't until he was thirty-nine years old that he was given a shot at the light-heavyweight title. He beat Joey Maxim by decision in 1955 and from then on remained undefeated in the light-heavyweight division. In the heavyweight division he famously floored the undefeated World Heavyweight Champion, Rocky Marciano, in the second round of their contest in September 1955, although he eventually lost the fight in the ninth round. Incredibly, he was forty-nine years old when he lost to Ali in 1962, and retired a year later.

Hugely popular out of the ring and everywhere praised for his charm and great sense of humor, Moore was a talented character actor and notably played the role of the runaway slave, Jim, in the 1960 film adaptation of *The Adventures of Huckleberry Finn.* He was also a respected trainer, working with such greats as Ali and Foreman. In retirement, he used his fame to support African American causes and set up the youth charity ABC (Any Boy Can) to help underprivileged children. In 1965, was awarded the key to the city of San Diego, California—his adopted home, where he died from heart failure in 1998, four days before his eighty-second birthday.

ERNIE TERRELL (B. 1939)

Ernie Terrell was born in Belzoni, Mississippi, and had nine siblings including younger sister Jean, who was to become the lead singer of The Supremes in the early 1970s. His family moved to Chicago where Ernie started boxing when he was fourteen. In 1957, he won the Chicago Golden Gloves Tournament at light heavyweight with a first round knockout.

He had fifty-five professional fights with forty-six wins (twenty-one KOs) and nine losses (two KOs). He defeated some notable contenders, including Cleveland Williams, Zora Folley, and George Chuvalo. He is most famous for his ugly fifteen-round clash with Ali on February 6, 1967. He retired later that year following an upset twelve-round decision in his fight with Thad Spencer in Houston, Texas, and a ten-round upset against Manuel Ramos in Mexico City, where the referee gave the victory to Ramos despite the fact that Terrell clearly dominated throughout the fight. Terrell decided to quit boxing to pursue a career in music—his other great passion.

In 1971, however, he made a comeback winning six straight fights. In 1973, Terrell made an unsuccessful attempt to secure the vacant National Americas Heavyweight title but, yet again, the referee gave the victory to his opponent, Chuck Wepner, despite the fact that Terrell had clearly dominated. There was no such doubt in Terrell's next and final fight however, where he was KO'd in the first round by Jeff Merritt in New York City. Terrell retired from boxing for good to become a record producer in Chicago.

CHUCK WEPNER (B. 1939)

Born in New York, Wepner grew up on the streets of Bayonne, New Jersey, living with his mother and brother on the East Forty-Ninth Street projects. He began boxing in the United States Marine Corps in 1956, and worked as a bouncer before turning professional in 1964. His first ten professional bouts were all in New York.

He fought fifty-one professional fights with thirty-five wins (seventeen KOs), fourteen Losses (nine KOs) and two draws. Although undoubtedly a boxing journeyman, he fought some true greats, including Sonny Liston and George Foreman, losing to both but knocking Foreman down in the second round. He is most famous for knocking down Ali in the ninth round of their 1975 world heavyweight title fight. It was rumored that Sylvester Stallone watched the fight with Ali at home and was inspired by Wepner's gutsy performance to write the script for Rocky. On his website, a picture of Wepner with Stallone and Robert DeNiro is labeled "good buddies."

A heavy drinker and self-confessed drug abuser and womanizer, Wepner served thee years of a ten-year prison sentence for possession of drugs in 1986. Today, the "Real Rocky" still lives in Bayonne with his wife, Linda, just across the river from the city where he was born.

LARRY HOLMES (1949–)

Born in Cuthbert, Georgia, Holmes was the fourth of twelve children. He and his family moved to Easton, Pennsylvania, in 1956, where he began boxing at the local Police Athletic League (PAL) center. He dropped out of school in the seventh grade to help support his family, initially working in a car wash.

He turned professional in 1973 and gained invaluable experience by sparring with Muhammed Ali, Joe Frazier, and Earnie Shavers. With his immense left jab, he won his first fort-eight professional bouts, just one short of Rocky Marciano's record consecutive victories in the heavyweight division. Victory over big hitter Earnie Shavers earned Holmes a shot at the WBC title against Ken Norton in June 1978. Holmes won the title by a fifteen-round decision in what has been described as one of the greatest heavyweight bouts of all time. He defended his title with seventeen straight wins, defeating such greats as Mike Weaver, Earnie Shavers, Leon Spinks, and Trevor Berbick. He was the WBC Heavyweight Champion from 1978 to 1983 and the IBF Heavyweight Champion from 1983 to 1985. His reign ended with a loss to Michael Spinks in a fifteen-round decision. He retired in 1986 after losing a rematch with Spinks.

He was lured back into the ring in 1988, at age thirty-eight, to fight the then-undisputed champion Mike Tyson. Holmes was knocked out in the fourth round—the first and only time he was knocked down in his career. He attempted without success to regain the title two more times: against Evander Holyfield in 1992 and Oliver McCall in 1995. He retired for good when he was fifty-two years old, going out on a high by defeating Eric Esch. His final professional record was seventy-five fights with sixty-nine wins (forty-four KOs) and six losses (one KO).

A brilliant entrepreneur, by the mid-1980s Holmes had established a business empire that included a five-story office building on Larry Holmes Drive in Easton and a restaurant called the Larry Holmes Ringside Restaurant, which he often visits to greet his customers. He is renowned as a philanthropist and was inducted into the Boxing Hall of Fame in 2008.

TUNNEY HUNSAKER (1930–2005)

Hunsaker was born in Caldwell County, Kentucky, and was named after the former World Heavyweight Champion Gene Tunney. He embarked on his boxing career while serving in the U.S. Air Force where he won a Golden Gloves title while stationed at Lackland Air Force Base in Texas.

Hunsaker's professional record stood at thirty-three fights with seventeen wins (eight KOs), fifteen defeats (7 KOs), and one draw, fighting such notables as Ernie Terrell, Tom McNeeley, and Alejandro Lavorante. In his final fight against Joe Sheldon on April 6, 1962, he was knocked out in ten rounds and went into a coma for nine days. Hunsaker is famous for being Ali's first professional opponent, and the two men became lifelong friends.

At the time he fought Ali, Hunsaker was the Police Chief of Fayetteville, West Virginia—a position he held for thirty-eight years. He was the youngest police chief in the history of West Virginia and was inducted into the Law Enforcement Hall of Fame. He even had a bridge named after him (former U.S. Route 19 Bridge crossing the New River Gorge). He died in West Virginia at the age of seventy-four following a long battle with Alzheimer's disease.

INDEX

ACKNOWLEDGMENTS AND CREDITS

This is for my dad, John Hajeski, who taught me that winning a fight matters less than fighting to win.

- Nancy Hajeski

ACKNOWLEDGMENTS

I would like to thank the design team of Brian MacMullen and Holly Lee as well as the editorial guidance of Lisa Purcell.

The author and publisher also offer thanks to those closely involved in the creation of this book: Moseley Road president Sean Moore; general manager Karen Prince; art director Brian MacMullen; editorial director Lisa Purcell; designer Holly Lee, and editors Ward Calhoun, Damien Moore and Jennifer Hamilton

CREDITS

All photographs from Getty Images except for the following:
Flip Schulke: cover and page 35
Library of Congress: pages 14, 15, 29, 31, 32
Photofest: pages 13, 37, 77, 184, 220
Wikipedia: page 12

"I got into the ring with Muhammad Ali once and I had him worried for a while. He thought he'd killed me!"

— TOMMY COOPER, COMEDIAN